A KICKASS GUIDE
TO FINDING CONFIDENCE
IN SPORT

SHOOT
FOR THE
STARS

DANIELLE BROWN

JAYDE PERKIN AND
FILIGRANA DE IDEAS

"My teacher thought I'd like volleyball, but I wasn't sure at first. I didn't know anyone who did it and I didn't think I was sporty enough to join the school club. I'm glad I tried it because I'm actually quite good at it and I've made loads of friends."

Izzy, age 11

"At school, girls aren't allowed to join the football club. This is unfair, and the boys say it's because we aren't good enough. I'm going to keep going until they realise that I deserve to be there, and I have complained to try and get this changed."

Isla, age 11

"When my body started changing, I was tired all the time, and I didn't want to exercise. If I didn't do very well it felt like I was failing at everything, but I'm glad I stuck with netball because it clears my mind, and my body feels better afterwards."

Patience, age 14

"I used to beat myself up if my PE teacher pointed out my mistakes. Even though she was trying to help me get better, I worried that I was really bad so I didn't try as hard or enjoy it as much. It's important to stop sometimes and remember the positives."

Yasmin, age 10

"I love sport, but my parents say I have to focus on my schoolwork instead. They don't think sport will help me be successful in the future."

Elif, age 12

"I sometimes think I'm not good enough, especially when I compare myself to others. I forget that they've been doing the sport much longer than me and it knocks my confidence. I've started focusing on myself and blurring out what everyone else is doing, and I'm enjoying it much more."

Erin, age 15

For my parents, Liz and Duncan, who always told me there
was no such thing as can't. You helped me to dream big,
explore my passions and smash through barriers – and these
messages still encourage me to keep chasing my dreams.

DB

Thank you to both Bristol Cooperative Gym and
LHG runclub, who've created supportive communities
around exercise. They've taught me how to love sports,
and appreciate the benefits of moving my body,
both physically and mentally.

And thank you to my 'little' brother Ty; my rock, my PT.
Who always gets me out and moving, even when it's wet,
or cold, or I'm tired. And I never regret it.

JP

Las Marías

FDI

LiTTLE TiGER
LONDON

LITTLE TIGER
An imprint of Little Tiger Press Limited
1 Coda Studios, 189 Munster Road, London SW6 6AW
www.littletiger.co.uk
Imported into the EEA by Penguin Random House Ireland,
Morrison Chambers, 32 Nassau Street, Dublin D02 YH68
www.littletigerpress.com
First published in Great Britain 2025
Text copyright © 2025 Danielle Brown
Illustrations copyright © 2025 Jayde Perkin and Filigrana de Ideas
Team Talk graphics © 2025, Shutterstock.com
A CIP catalogue record for this book is available from the British Library
All rights reserved • Printed in China
ISBN: 978-1-83891-665-7 • CPB/1800/2964/0125
10 9 8 7 6 5 4 3 2 1

FSC
www.fsc.org
MIX
Paper | Supporting
responsible forestry
FSC® C020056

The Forest Stewardship Council® (FSC®)
is a global, not-for-profit organisation
dedicated to the promotion of responsible
forest management worldwide. FSC® defines
standards based on agreed principles for
responsible forest stewardship that are
supported by environmental, social,
and economic stakeholders.
To learn more, visit www.fsc.org

A KICKASS GUIDE
TO FINDING CONFIDENCE
IN SPORT

SHOOT
FOR THE
STARS

Danielle Brown

Jayde Perkin and
Filigrana de Ideas

CONTENTS

WELCOME!

This book is perfect for you if you love sport (or feel a bit curious about it) because it's all about sport and how to get better at it. More importantly, it's about how to have fun doing it, because being brilliant isn't about winning big. Whether you watch it, dabble in it, compete or coach, sport is an exciting way to unwind and have a great time. You might be happiest having a go with your friends or dream of succeeding on the big stage – however you choose to play sport, it opens the door to unforgettable moments and incredible opportunities.

And hey, if you've picked this at random and you're not sure whether sport is your thing, you are most welcome here! There is, as we'll find out, a sport for everyone, and sometimes it takes a bit of time to discover the one that makes your heart sing.

TOGETHER, WE CAN HELP YOU FIND IT.

I spent almost ten years as an elite athlete, where I achieved many world records, world firsts and world titles. (Yes, it takes me ages to polish my trophy cabinet!) Now I'm retired, I have the great privilege of helping others. I love visiting schools and telling my story, and over the years many girls have shared their worries, fears, aspirations and experiences with me.

"I'm a bit nervous about trying triathlon because my friends don't want to do it."

"I don't like doing PE because I have to wear shorts."

"I want to do rugby, but I got told it's too rough for girls."

Nobody – and I mean nobody –
should ever feel like they don't belong,
that they aren't good enough,
or that their dreams aren't important.

Now, I may come from a competitive background, but that doesn't mean I think this is the right path for everyone. You might want to represent your country at the Olympic or Paralympic Games, go on an adventure, make new friends, volunteer as a coach, learn a new skill, keep fit and healthy or just have some fun.

With so many sporty options, it can be tricky to know where to start. Together, we'll explore different ways you can get involved with sport, uncover your superpower strengths and build the success skills needed to strike it big. We're going to learn from some sensational athletes who take the word 'inspiring' to the next level.

We'll get to grips with how to look after your body to perform well AND feel brilliantly confident about being you.

And, of course, we're going to talk about how to smash through challenges. Sport is meant to be fun, but that doesn't mean it won't get tough at times. You are not alone, even if it feels that way sometimes. This book is here to help if you have a bad day, your motivation runs dry, you meet a doubter or have a nasty little voice inside your head chipping away at your confidence. There is always, always a way around challenges if you look in the right place.

SO, LET'S DO THIS!

IT'S TIME TO FALL IN LOVE WITH SPORT AND BECOME AWESOME AT BEING YOU.

© Danielle Brown

"Technique and ability alone do not get you to the top: it is the WILLPOWER that is most important."

SPORT: Alpinism

COUNTRY: Japan

JUNKO TABEI

On 16 May 1975, Junko Tabei from Japan stood on top of Mount Everest, the tallest peak in the world. It was a breathtaking moment, worth every step of the long journey to get there.

She fell in love with mountain climbing on a school trip at the age of ten. Her parents couldn't afford to send her on expeditions, so she waited until she was at university to pursue it seriously. When she said she was going to climb Everest people laughed. "It's impossible for a woman to do that," they told her, and she found it hard to raise funds.

But Junko never thought about giving up. She taught piano lessons to pay for the trip and made her climbing clothes from old curtains. Last-minute sponsorship came from a Japanese newspaper, and she began the climb with her team. Despite being hurt in an avalanche on the ascent, Junko pressed on to become the first woman in the world to stand on the summit.

YOUR SPORT IS OUT THERE

TAKE A SHOT AT:

Falling in love with sport. The fun factor is the reason we keep turning up to play, try our hardest and persevere when it gets tough, so let's discover how to find the sport that brings us happiness and keeps our motivation levels high.

We sometimes hear stories of athletes who discovered their sport when they were infants. Sky Brown was pulling off jaw-dropping tricks on a skateboard by the time she was three. Serena Williams started playing tennis at the same age. Simone Biles took her first gymnastics lesson at six.

AND THEN THERE ARE PEOPLE LIKE ME . . .

MY STORY

I didn't fall in love with a single sport. I wanted to try them all, so I put my name down for every sports club at my school. Cross country, table tennis, hockey, sign me up. I got to make new friends, soak in magnificent views from the top of mountains and enjoy the thrill of competition. I wasn't terribly talented at any of these sports, but that didn't matter. It wasn't as if I was planning a career in it . . .

This all changed when I was eleven. My feet began to hurt after I'd been running: no big deal to begin with, but the pain got worse and it wouldn't go away. Eventually I was diagnosed with a condition called Complex Regional Pain Syndrome (CRPS for short). I went from being the kid who tried everything to not doing sport at all, and it felt like part of myself had been ripped out. If I wanted sport to be in my life now I was disabled, I had to think about it differently.

© Danielle Brown

I'd heard about archery and on my fifteenth birthday I started a beginner's course with my dad.

It was just like every other sport I'd tried – I was rubbish at it! I couldn't hit the target to save my life, never mind the middle of it, but I wasn't there to shatter world records. I was there to have some fun – and WOW! It was fun! Hours melted away as I shot arrow after arrow and when my first lesson ended, I couldn't wait to do it again.

I had found my sport.

The club coaches were full of encouragement. As I searched for my arrows with the club's trusty metal detector, I'm not entirely sure what they saw, but they believed in my abilities and I went along with it. I worked hard, pouring my energy and enthusiasm into it. Every personal best reaffirmed this – I had potential and one day I was going to reach it.

I made the Great Britain team three years later.

I earned my place on the national team through hard work, though 'work' makes it sound horribly boring. How about we call it hard fun instead? Here's how it worked: the more I practised the better I got, the better I got the more I enjoyed it, and the more I enjoyed it the more I wanted to practise. I loved archery so much that I didn't complain about getting up super early to go to competitions (well, not much anyway), or training in the rain.

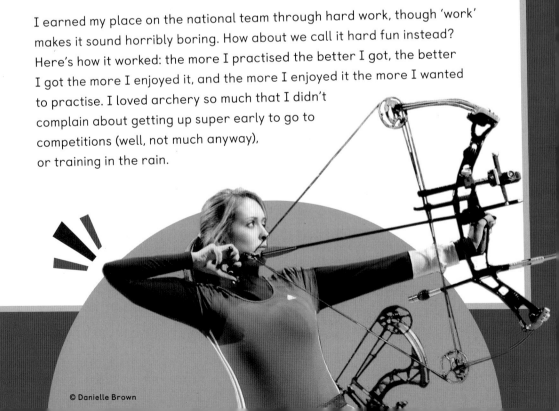

© Danielle Brown

CREATING YOUR SPORTS STORY

Every athlete has their own brilliant back story. They may have run, jumped, dived, swung, tumbled, fought, scored or saved their way into the record books, but each one took a different path to get there. Your life doesn't have to be turned upside down like mine to be set on the right track, nor do you need to know what your sport is from day dot. Some athletes tried many different sports before they found one they loved, some came across theirs by chance and others were discovered by coaches.

BUT THE WORST REASON TO GET INTO SPORT IS BECAUSE YOU HAVE TO . . .

We're told that exercise is good for us, and we're expected to get on with it. There are loads of things that are good for us, like eating all our greens and going to bed early. To fuel that fire inside we need something much more inspiring. Passion encourages us to give more today than we did yesterday and

The first rule of loving your sport and being totally awesome at it is: **FIND YOUR PASSION.**

gives us the courage to keep going through tough times. If Sky Brown hated spending time at the skate park, do you think she'd be the proud owner of an Olympic medal? She's overcome broken bones and worrying injuries, getting back on her board each time she falls because skating is her happy place.

BE BRAVE, BE STRONG, HAVE FUN AND DO IT BECAUSE

Two-time
Olympic **bronze medallist**
(2020 and 2024)

Youngest athlete to win
a medal for **Team GB** (2020)

Two-time **gold medallist** at
X Games Southern California
(2021 and 2022)

YOU LOVE IT!

Sky Brown, British-Japanese skateboarder and surfer

FINDING - AND KEEPING - YOUR PASSION

Even if you know that middle-distance running or underwater rugby (yes, that's an actual sport!) is your thing, having a go at loads of different sports can be fantastic fun.

It helps you develop extra skills, it can take away any pressure you might feel from doing just one sport and scientists have proved that athletes who play more than one sport stick with them for longer.

TALK ABOUT A WIN-WIN-WIN.

DID YOU KNOW?

Over 8,000 sports and games have been invented around the world! From karting to karate, there's a whole world of options and, among them, there's the perfect one (or two, or three, or . . .) for you.

FIND OUT WHAT FIRES YOU UP

It's time to turn detective, so let's start looking for clues that tell you more about your passions. Jot down answers for each step and add to them when you discover something new:

STEP 1

KNOWING WHAT SPORT (or sports) you like is a solid place to start. Write a list of sports and activities you enjoy (mine includes archery – obviously – and paddleboarding, scuba diving and wild camping) and sports you don't enjoy (working out at the gym and dance, for me).

Check out the handy list of sports at the end (page 168) if you'd like some inspiration.

STEP 2

TIME TO START DIGGING.

For the sports you don't like (or even the sports you do), what don't you like about them? A bad experience put you off, perhaps? A sport could be too competitive or not competitive enough. You might hate pushing your body, have fallen out with a teammate or not feel confident doing it in front of others.

> "Team sports aren't my favourite because I don't like letting my teammates down. I get bored doing drills without knowing why and I don't like watching sport on the telly. I'd much rather be playing it."

STEP 3

© Danielle Brown

NOW FOR THE BIG ONE:

What do you like best about sport?

- Do you have fun with your friends or want to make a difference in your community?
- Do you like getting fitter, faster or stronger?
- Maybe you dream of winning medals?

BEBE VIO

AWESOME ATHLETE

Beatrice Vio loved fencing more than anything else in the world. She started at a local club when she was five years old and dreamed of going to the Olympics, but six years later a deadly strain of meningitis meant her legs and arms had to be amputated.

The first thing she wanted to know when she came out of hospital was when she could fence again. Everybody told her it was impossible but Bebe refused to listen.

Fencing was her passion, and she was determined to find a way to do it. With specially designed prosthetic arms she learned how to fence again and dominated her competition, winning a gold medal at the Rio 2016 Paralympic Games and retaining her title in Tokyo 2020.

Bebe now campaigns for better access to vaccinations. If she had been given a vaccine, she would not have become ill with meningitis. She uses her platform to raise awareness and support other young people.

"Everything is impossible at the beginning."

SPORT: Fencing
COUNTRY: Italy

21

SPOT THE DIFFERENCE

Without passion, your motivation is out of here. Sure, we all have those days where **EVERYTHING** feels like a drag and the last thing you want is to get down to training. This happens for all sorts of reasons – like feeling tired or stressed – but it's a good idea to check whether any of your likes or dislikes have changed. Friction with a new coach or a teammate, for example, can make you feel miserable. Once you know why you're not enjoying it as much you can try to find a way to fix it.

YOU CAN TELL WHEN SOMEBODY HAS FOUND THEIR PASSION:

Their eyes gleam when they talk about it, and you can hear the excitement in their voice. Getting a clearer idea of what you love about sport helps you keep your passion once you've found it.

© Halfpoint, Shutterstock, 2022

A CHANGE OF DIRECTION

There came a point when I fell out of love with archery. Eight years as world number one is a pretty cool feat but making sure I stayed there became so stressful. My life was all about winning and somewhere along the way I forgot how to have fun. Anxiety chased me from event to event, where I felt I had to be perfect.

Sometimes we need to take a step back and realise that our energy is better spent elsewhere. This can be tricky, causing questions and worries. Is it the right choice? What if I'm better just sticking it out? I wrestled with this decision for a long time. Archery had been a big part of my life for so long and it was difficult to admit that it might be time for a change. My social life was tied into it, my way of life was built around it and I couldn't imagine walking away from the sport that had given me so much.

From the ashes of that dying passion came a brand new one. Sport is still important to me, and I channelled this enthusiasm into helping others which is the **BEST** feeling in the world. From mentoring aspiring young athletes to using sport to make the world a more equal place for girls and disabled people, I am enjoying sport on my terms and it feels awesome inside. I still do archery for fun, though I can't say I've completely lost my competitive streak . . .

YOUR GUIDING STAR

Passion is a feeling. Some feelings stick around for the long haul, whilst others change over time. You can be really into a sport and then lose interest in it – and this is okay – as long as it's for the right reason.

THE RIGHT REASON:

Leaving a sport behind because you've found a new one or discovered something else that challenges you, intrigues you, pushes you, excites you and sparks that fire inside you.

THE NOT-AT-ALL-RIGHT REASON:

Worrying about what others think of us is completely natural and it's also completely unhelpful. If we feel pressure to act a certain way or to like certain things, it can lead to choices that don't make us very happy. If we're not careful, we could end up missing out on a brilliant opportunity to try something new, or – uh oh – walking away from something that, deep down, we love doing.

If you ever have to answer these tough questions, go back to finding out what fires you up (page 18) and use your answers like a guiding star. Let them help make some of those tricky decisions a little easier. Also, talk about it with the people in your support network. You are not expected to make big decisions alone . . .

If you're feeling pressured or torn between different passions, advice from others might clear things up.

Life feels great when you're doing something that makes you happy. And remember, there is no need to find your sport straight away.

THIS IS ALL PART OF THE JOURNEY AND ALL PART OF THE FUN.

"KEEP BEING YOU, AND KEEP HAVING FUN WITH WHAT YOU'RE DOING."

Mo'ne Davis

YOU CAN'T DO THAT!

TAKE A SH★T AT:

Saying, "I can". There might be moments where you doubt yourself, or feel you ought to behave a certain way or like particular sports because that's what others expect. You can learn how to tune these doubts out and keep doing the sports that bring you joy.

THE RISE OF WOMEN'S SPORT

Sport is for everybody, which definitely means you! We live in a time where women's sport is becoming more popular; where it is possible to watch it, play it and slay it, but this wasn't always the case. Nope, for centuries women wanting to enjoy sport have had a sour deal.

"GIRLS HAVE NO BUSINESS BEING IN SPORTS."

From ancient Greek gymnasiums to Victorian running tracks, people have long thought (very wrongly!) that women were too weak for exercise. That they were too delicate to get sweaty, grimy and muddy and too fragile to push themselves hard. For years women's sport existed on the edge, but thanks to the determination and bravery of trailblazing women who refused to take no for an answer, this has changed.

In 1900, women were only allowed to compete in five sports at the Olympic Games. French rower Alice Milliat campaigned for more women's events to be added. When the International Olympic Committee (IOC) refused, she organised her own international competitions for women.

Athletes travelled from all over the world to compete, as did thousands of spectators, and the IOC eventually changed their minds. Women were finally allowed to compete in gymnastics and athletics in 1928, and in Paris 2024, over 100 years since Alice first started her campaign, there were an equal number of female and male athletes competing at an Olympic Games for the very first time.

Laws that stopped women and girls from taking part in all kinds of sports, from marathon-running to boxing, got updated and, more importantly, so did attitudes. Today, television viewing figures all over the world are shooting up, stadiums are selling out and women's participation is bigger than ever before.

Not all the cobwebby old thoughts have been swept away, but just because they haven't been consigned to the history books (yet!) doesn't mean you must live your life by them. It takes time for changing ideas to be fully accepted.

"AS WE HAVE NO VOTE, WE CANNOT MAKE OUR NEEDS PUBLICLY FELT, OR BRING PRESSURE TO BEAR IN THE RIGHT QUARTERS. I ALWAYS TELL MY GIRLS THAT THE VOTE IS ONE OF THE THINGS THEY WILL HAVE TO WORK FOR IF FRANCE IS TO KEEP ITS PLACE WITH THE OTHER NATIONS IN THE REALM OF FEMININE SPORT."

Alice Milliat

DID YOU KNOW?

Football is one of the most popular games in the world, but for years women were banned from playing professionally. After World War I, women's football drew record crowds and the English FA worried it would take focus from the men's game and lead women down an 'unsuitable' path. In 1921 they refused to let women play on their grounds, and this rule stayed in place until 1971.

At the 2023 FIFA Women's World Cup, England goalkeeper Mary Earps was upset to learn that fans could not buy her football shirt. Nike made other players' shirts, but they claimed they hadn't made any goalkeeper jerseys because they didn't think anybody would want to buy them, despite having made them for the men's world cup the year before.

> "I CAN'T REALLY SUGAR-COAT THIS IN ANY WAY, SO I'M NOT GOING TO TRY. IT IS HUGELY DISAPPOINTING AND VERY HURTFUL."

Mary Earps, MBE

29

When 16-year-old Emmy Somauroo started a petition, it quickly gained lots of signatures. This outcry from fans was so powerful that Nike reversed their decision, bringing out limited editions of Mary's shirt which sold out in less than a day.

MY STORY

I signed up for football practice in my first week at secondary school. The empty changing room echoed as I pulled on my PE kit, hoping the other girls were running late. Nobody else turned up and I walked outside, alone.

It turned out that football was very popular, just not with the girls. Over thirty boys crowded around the PE block. "Time for the warm-up. Get into pairs and we'll jog around the pitch," barked the PE teacher.

The boys moved away from me quickly. "I don't want to be stuck with the girl," one guy hissed. I pretended I hadn't heard and turned towards another boy. "I'm with him," he said, pointing at the partner he'd miraculously found.

This carried on until there were only two of us left and the PE teacher stepped in, ushering us together much to the boy's dismay. When it was time for the game, things didn't get better. Nobody wanted me on their team. Nobody passed the ball to me. I trotted up and down the pitch, waving my arms and yelling to my teammates as I heard them say:

"She shouldn't be here."

"Girls can't play football."

"I can't believe she thinks she's one of us."

It's a horrible feeling to find yourself in a place where you aren't accepted or celebrated for all the brilliant things you can give. I wish I had been stronger. I wish I'd shrugged off the comments and catcalls and stood my ground. But it's easy to look back and wish you'd done things differently.

This experience was just one of many, a tiny square in a giant patchwork, and it played a part in helping me become who I am today. The places we play sport should feel safe and welcoming and, if they don't, something needs to change. I learned how to be strong and stand up for myself to stop other girls, like you, being put off sport.

Thankfully, things have come a long way since the days I was speeding around a PE hall, and we now hear about far more female athletes totally bossing it and taking the world by storm. Football, in particular, has seen a massive surge in popularity. Over 16.6 million girls worldwide are tearing it up on the pitch!

YAY!

IT'S YOUR CHOICE

The only person who gets to choose what your sporting goals are and how you exercise is **you**. This doesn't stop some people from trying though. Unhelpful opinions such as,

"YOU CAN'T DO THAT!"

can tear us down and might influence what sport we choose and whether we continue doing something we enjoy.

BOXED IN

Some people like to put others in neat little boxes.

Putting somebody in a box means making all kinds of assumptions about them based on what they look like on the outside, without knowing who they are on the inside.

It describes the things they like, the things they are good at and how they behave.

DID YOU KNOW?
The invention of the bicycle gave women more freedom – and it was a great excuse to ditch their petticoats! Not everybody liked this, leading to the spread of bizarre (and totally untrue) rumours that cycling could cause women dangerous health problems.

In the gendered box, girls like pink, they're good at art and reading, and they're caring, sensitive and weaker than boys. These assumptions are known as stereotypes.

Boys aren't left out, mind: they've got their very own box. It says they like blue, are good at maths and sports, are strong and brave and do not cry. **Ever.**

Can you see the problem here? Defining what we should and shouldn't do changes the way people see us and the way we see ourselves. We might feel like we need to act a certain way to fit in – like pretending we want to do an activity we aren't interested in or not going back to football club because we don't feel welcome.

The worst thing is that stereotypes are based on limited experiences, so can never be true for everyone. Whatever your gender, you can be sensitive, caring, kind, tough and smart. You can laugh and cry, have awesome adventures, aspire to achieve big things and enjoy all kinds of sports.

33

PEOPLE WOULD SAY, "GIRLS DON'T PLAY HOCKEY. GIRLS DON'T SKATE."

Five-time
Olympic medallist
(four gold and one silver)

Seven-time World
Championship **gold medallist**

Canada's **all-time leader**
in international
goals

I WOULD SAY, "WATCH THIS."

Hayley Wickenheiser, Canadian former ice hockey player

LET'S SMASH SOME STEREOTYPES

I learned a marvellous trick
to stop stereotypes tearing me down.
Whenever somebody tells me I can't do
something or I get a limiting thought about
myself, I like to picture myself breaking out
of the box they are trying to trap me in.
I grab my imaginary bat and I take
a swing at those words with
a response of my own.

Girls aren't as good at sport?

SMASH!

I'll show you just how
awesome girls are at sport.

Nobody cares about women's sport?

HA!

Tell that to the millions of athletes,
coaches and fans around the world.

I catch like a girl?

THWACK!

I bet you wish you could
catch like a girl too!

ACTIVITY

BREAK OUT OF THAT BOX

Can you try this with a negative comment you've heard? Imagine yourself whacking those words into orbit with a sports racket of your choosing. Hit it as hard as you can and feel those words shattering into a thousand tiny pieces.

IT FEELS SO GOOD WHEN THOSE WALLS START TO COME DOWN.

TEAM TALK

If negative comments upset you, don't bottle it up. Thoughts and feelings can get a bit muddled up inside, and talking about them with someone you trust can help you make sense of them. They might be able to offer some stonking advice, come up with ideas to tackle the issue or simply help you feel better.

YOU ARE NOT ALONE

Whatever challenges women and girls often face, it's important not to assume that bad experiences lie ahead. Without the kindness of many, many people, I wouldn't have achieved a fraction of my successes. You should never think that there isn't a place for you in sport (there totally is), or that you don't deserve to be there (you totally do).

And you are not alone.

Many athletes have tirelessly fought to make the world a better place and their actions have caused a change. It hasn't been easy, but each voice, each win, each decision to defy the doubters, created a tiny ripple that has spread and turned into a wave as people all over the world join in.

SPORT: Weightlifting

COUNTRY: Pakistan/USA

38

"We may look different but we have the same goals of unity, freedom, and social harmony. I hope people will become more accepting and tolerant of each other. I very much appreciated the show of support and encouragement from my fellow athletes."

KULSOOM ABDULLAH

Kulsoom Abdullah never planned to be a weightlifter, but she ended up changing the sport forever. She wanted to get stronger for her Taekwondo classes so she gave weightlifting a try.

Two years later she was invited to compete at the national championships, but she was not allowed to cover her arms and legs or wear a hijab, which went against her religious beliefs. Kulsoom asked for this to change, but USA Weightlifting said 'no'.

Instead of giving up, she spoke out. She did not attend the national championships that year, but took her fight to the media and her story spread far and wide.

She then approached the International Weightlifting Federation with the media behind her, and the rule was changed, enabling her to compete. That same year she also represented Pakistan at the World Championships.

Thanks to her stance, other sports also changed their rules, allowing more athletes to compete whilst staying true to their beliefs. Now, Kulsoom wants to inspire other girls to break through outdated stereotypes – just because they can.

YOU ARE STRONG, BRAVE AND FEARLESS

Not everyone you meet will understand your ambitions, passions or dreams. There will always be doubters and non-believers who try their hardest to put others down. But you know what? We don't have to listen to them . . .

It sucks if we are treated differently or have our dreams stomped on, but I know that you are strong. Deep inside, there is a will forged in iron, a stubborn streak that doesn't show itself until it is needed. Like Kulsoom Abdullah, you have the courage to fight for what you believe in and say:

"I WANT THIS AND I KNOW I CAN ACHIEVE IT. IF YOU'RE WITH ME, GREAT! IF NOT, THAT WON'T STOP ME."

WE NEVER KNOW WHAT WE ARE **CAPABLE** OF UNTIL WE START TO **EXPLORE**.

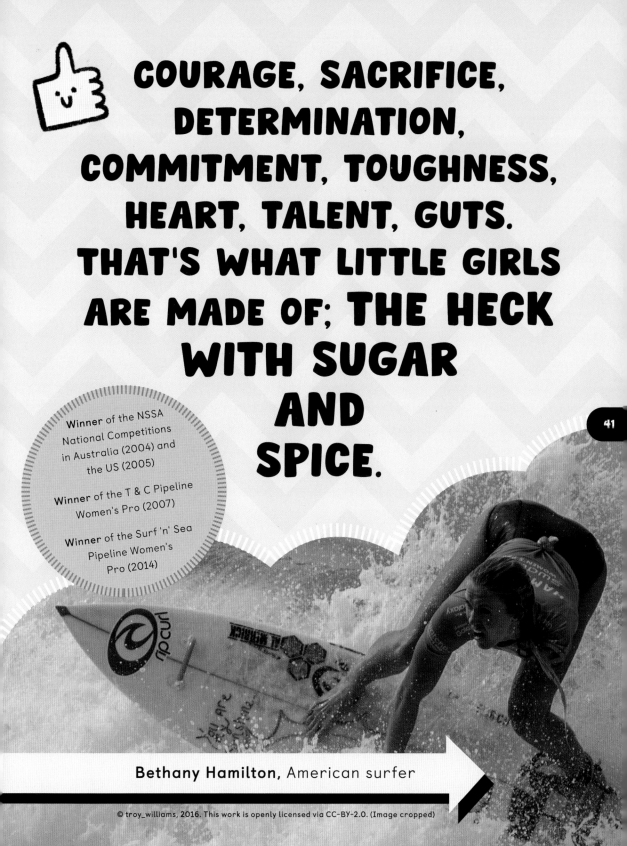

COURAGE, SACRIFICE, DETERMINATION, COMMITMENT, TOUGHNESS, HEART, TALENT, GUTS. THAT'S WHAT LITTLE GIRLS ARE MADE OF; THE HECK WITH SUGAR AND SPICE.

Winner of the NSSA National Competitions in Australia (2004) and the US (2005)

Winner of the T & C Pipeline Women's Pro (2007)

Winner of the Surf 'n' Sea Pipeline Women's Pro (2014)

41

Bethany Hamilton, American surfer

LOVE YOUR BODY

TAKE A SHOT AT:

Loving and caring for your body, feeding it the right messages so you don't miss out on the things you enjoy. This involves listening to what your body needs and exercising at your pace.

I live by the motto:

TO GET THE MOST OUT OF MYSELF AS AN **ATHLETE**, I FIRST HAVE TO GET THE MOST OUT OF MYSELF AS A **PERSON**.

Getting better as an athlete wasn't about spending more time shooting arrows or hitting the gym harder. It was about looking after myself and finding out what I needed to thrive. Learning to love my body for all its wonderful fragilities and quirks was a big part of this.

Many bodies throw up additional things to think about. Hormone levels fluctuate, and for those with a monthly cycle this can affect everything from strength to energy levels and mood. This doesn't mean that these delightfully complicated bodies of ours can't achieve exceptional things though . . .

In 2019, ultra-long-distance runner Jasmin Paris smashed the world record for the Winter Spine Race, a gruelling 431km (268mi) across hilly terrain. Her time of 83 hours and 12 minutes was over 12 hours faster than the men's world record!

What makes this achievement even more impressive is that during her rest breaks she pumped breast milk. Some 14 months after having a baby, her body was still adapting to big hormonal changes, but it didn't stop her from doing the sport that brought her so much joy – and doing it really well!

> **"DO WHAT YOU FEEL IS RIGHT AND WHAT MAKES YOU HAPPY."**
>
> Jasmin Paris, MBE

MY STORY

One day I was living life and having fun, and the next . . . **BAM**, puberty hit.

Suddenly, I was catapulted into centre stage, as if a spotlight was following every move I made and people were watching me all the time. If I made a mistake, everyone would see, laugh and think less of me.

When it felt like the entire world was judging me, doing ordinary stuff like dribbling a hockey ball was harder. And doing it in a PE skirt made it a million times worse. If the wind blew the wrong way, or I tripped and flashed my class it would be the most embarrassing thing EVER!

This new awareness – and awkwardness – about my body was weird. I didn't notice any of the good stuff. Oh no, my brain zoomed in on my flaws and failings. Having CRPS made these feelings even more believable. We all have differences, but I worried that mine made me stand out, made me less 'normal'. I didn't fit in with the picture-perfect bodies plastered everywhere I looked, and I thought I never would.

Yet my hopes, my passions and my dreams for the future won out. They were stronger than my fears because, despite the hang-ups and the pressures, I fed myself the right messages. I learned to love my body for its strength and courage and abilities. I know your hopes and dreams can win too. Every time you try something new, speak kindly about yourself or give maximum effort, you're getting one step closer.

Learning anything new takes time. It's okay to feel overwhelmed every now and again as you discover more about your amazing body. It's definitely okay to celebrate the mini milestones and give yourself a high five for hanging in there on the tough days. Most importantly, it's okay to keep believing in yourself and having fun. It's normal for your body to feel a bit strange and different as it goes through all these changes, but this doesn't have to change your love for sport.

DID YOU KNOW?
Females outperform males in ultra-endurance sports. During super long-distance races, our bodies don't tire as quickly due to our muscle fibres and how we burn fat.

THE UPS AND DOWNS OF PUBERTY

Our bodies are truly incredible, powering us to new heights and proving that our potential is limitless.

Growing up is an exciting time, but puberty also gives us a whole heap of new challenges, confusions and considerations. It's also a time of new experiences, where we begin to figure out who we are and what we want from life. During puberty your body gets flooded with lots of different hormones, helping it to transition into adulthood. It grows much faster than before, changes shape, begins to smell a little different. You may start getting periods. All of this can take a bit of getting used to, especially as these changes feel like they're happening quicker than the 100m sprint.

Often it's not change itself that can cause us to worry but the uncertainty that it brings. When we understand what's happening to our body it's like switching on the light so we can see exactly what we're dealing with.

FLIPPING YOUR FOCUS

Body image is the way you see your body and how you feel about it. Whilst it isn't always easy to be body-positive, there are many reasons to feel good about yourself.

However, if we compare the areas we feel insecure about with somebody else's highlight reel we're always going to fall short.

What we're seeing may not be real (filters have a lot to answer for!) and that person who looks super chill on the outside might not be feeling the same way on the inside.

Comparing ourselves unfavourably to others causes us to forget our own amazing abilities and achievements and it can drain our self-esteem.

I ♥ MY BODY

The not-so-good news is that your brain doesn't come with an off switch. It's not going to stop comparing just because you tell it to. However, you can outsmart your brain! Yes, by teaching it to compare in a healthier way you can sidestep a lot of negativity.

MY BRILLIANT BODY CAN . . .

Instead of looking outwards and trying to measure yourself against another person, look inwards.

Are you faster than you were last year, last month or last week? Are you stronger, fitter or more motivated?

Even if you find it hard to be comfortable in your body, focusing on what it CAN do is a powerful hack. With all that growing, it deserves a break, so let's appreciate all the amazing things it does for you.

Grab your journal or notebook and finish this sentence with as many wonderful things as you can think of:

My brilliant body can . . .

48

TEAM TALK

If you're not feeling comfortable in your body you can talk to someone you trust, like a friend or grown-up, who can listen and offer support. With time, patience and help, you'll learn more about yourself and your body, and how to embrace who you are.

PERIODS AND SPORT

For many people, puberty will lead to periods, and this is a huge change that can throw up some extra things to think about.

Getting a period can be inconvenient at times, but it doesn't have to stop you from being active, delivering big results, or having fun. And for those who have periods, it just means looking after your body in a slightly different way.

COUNTRY: China
SPORT: Swimming

50

"If you do not give up on yourself there will always be somewhere you can shine."

FU YUANHUI

At an Olympic Games, only a handful of athletes come away with a medal and even fewer become a household name. Olympic swimmer Fu Yuanhui from China won the hearts of millions of fans in Rio 2016. She didn't break a world record or steal a jaw-dropping victory at the very last second. She talked about her period.

A reporter broke the news that she won a bronze medal in the backstroke and her surprise was glorious. "Huh?" she gasped. "I didn't know!" Beaming on the podium, her joy spread around the world.

A few days later, in the 4 x 100m medley relay, Fu hoped for another medal with her team but she did not swim as fast as before. The Chinese team finished in fourth place.

51

"My period started last night, so I'm feeling pretty weak and really tired," she explained in the post-race interview. People fell in love with Fu's refreshingly honest interviews. This was a real athlete who was not afraid to be unapologetically herself.

THE RIGHT TOOLS FOR THE JOB

Fu's admission started a very important conversation: periods can sometimes affect performance and it's okay to talk about it. After her race, many people reached out to say they didn't realise you could swim whilst you were on your period, which led to great suggestions about different period products available, such as tampons.

It's difficult to do a job properly without the right equipment. You can't show jump without a horse or curl without a broom, and it's hard to be active without the right period gear. It's normal to worry about people spotting your pad or that you'll leak. I get it. For years we had to wear white trousers in archery competitions, which was terrifying. It didn't matter whether my period was due or not – "What if it suddenly appears?" I worried as soon as I pulled them on.

TMI? There is no such thing as too much information! We don't need to feel embarrassed about bodies doing what they are meant to do. Some amazing athletes have talked about their experiences and inspired all kinds of ideas, like cleverly designed underwear that stops leaks, so you can feel secure. Darker-coloured clothing is also becoming popular, reducing anxiety around period leaks.

DID YOU KNOW?
Wimbledon has one of the strictest dress codes around – athletes must be dressed from head-to-toe in white or face a fine. In 2023, the tournament relaxed the rules after getting a lot of pressure from players and commentators, allowing women to wear dark coloured undershorts.

DOWNLOAD A PERIOD TRACKER

If you have periods, over time you'll get used to how that brilliant body of yours works throughout the different stages of your monthly cycle. Keeping a record lets you learn more about your body so you can take better care of it. There are some great apps out there, which help you understand what is 'normal' for you. At the start of puberty, it can take a while for your body to settle into a regular pattern, but you quickly learn what feels right and notice changes that seem out of whack.

SELF-CARE FOR SUCCESS

Enter self-care. The superhero of skills. It's an excellent way to make sure that all the changes that come with puberty, including periods if/when you get them, don't derail your dreams. Self-care is about taking care of your body and mind. The better we look after ourselves, the better we feel and the better we perform.

EXERCISE comes with the official stamp of approval from scientists. It might be the last thing you want to do on a period, especially if your energy levels have dipped, but when we exercise we get a rush of endorphins – our feel good hormone – which helps us to, well, feel good. It can also help with cramps if you get those.

TEAM TALK

Self-care is important all the time, not just when you're having an off day, or on the 2–7 days a month you might be on your period. Doing one thing for yourself every single day (like having a bubble bath, going for a run or reading a book) is a good habit to get into.

ZZZ

LISTEN TO YOUR BODY.
It will tell you what you need. Sometimes this means taking a day off to rest; other days you're up for a beast of a workout.

WARM UP AND COOL DOWN,
taking longer than you normally would if on a period. Your ligaments (the tissues that hold your body together) become stretchier during your period. It can make your arms and legs feel like spaghetti, so drills and skills might feel a bit weird. This form of self-care is important to prevent injuries, as well as helping you ease into your sport a bit more gently.

© Pressmaster, Shutterstock, 2024

BE KIND TO YOURSELF.
This doesn't mean hiding under the duvet and refusing to come out while having a period or raiding the cupboard and scoffing every chocolate biscuit in sight. Being kind is giving yourself positive encouragement and also telling yourself to keep persevering with your sport. Not in the 'beat yourself up' sort of way – that is never okay! Treat yourself the same way you would a friend: be gentle, patient and encouraging.

FINDING YOUR NORMAL

It is normal to gain a little weight during puberty. It's part of the various changes that happen at this time, but can take a bit of time to get used to. Doing more exercise to try and get rid of this weight is not the answer though.

When you exercise you spend energy, and to let the body recover properly you need to eat enough fuel (AKA food) to replace it. If we have too much energy going out (overexercising) and not enough energy going in (not eating enough) then our body doesn't have enough energy left over to grow and develop. This imbalance of energy is called RED-S and it can cause all kinds of health problems, including feeling tired, having weak bones and missing periods.

Whilst all bodies are different, it is not normal for periods to stop completely. This could be a sign that your body is working too hard and needs to slow down to refuel properly. It is difficult to know exactly how much food you need to eat to balance out your training, but listening to your body, your coaches and making sure that you fuel up before and after exercise is vital.

Remember, your normal is personal to you, but it's really important that you don't just 'put up with it' if you think that something isn't right.

Charlotte Henshaw MBE, superstar and British swimmer turned canoeist, has won Paralympic medals in both sports. In 2020, she was diagnosed with endometriosis, a very painful condition where the cells lining the uterus wall build up in other areas of the body. Some days she struggled to get out of bed.

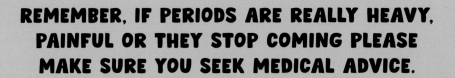

REMEMBER, IF PERIODS ARE REALLY HEAVY, PAINFUL OR THEY STOP COMING PLEASE MAKE SURE YOU SEEK MEDICAL ADVICE.

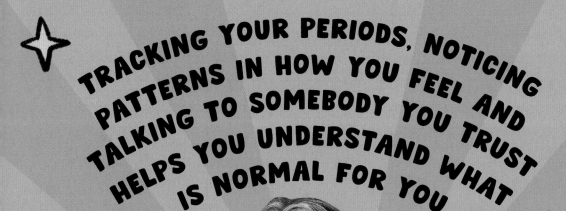

TRACKING YOUR PERIODS, NOTICING PATTERNS IN HOW YOU FEEL AND TALKING TO SOMEBODY YOU TRUST HELPS YOU UNDERSTAND WHAT IS NORMAL FOR YOU

Two-time Paralympic gold medallist in canoe (Tokyo 2020 and Paris 2024)

Two-time Paralympic medallist in swimming (silver at London 2012 and bronze at Rio 2016)

Two-time European champion in Para swimming

OR WHETHER THERE'S A PROBLEM. AND NEVER SUFFER IN SILENCE IF YOU'RE IN PAIN.

Charlotte Henshaw, MBE, British Paralympic swimmer and canoeist

FEELING CONFIDENT IN YOUR CLOTHES

Clothing has a super important job on the sports field: it needs to offer support in all the right places, be flexible enough to let you move freely and be tough enough to get the job done. Most of all, you need to feel comfortable in it.

Sometimes the kit we're asked to wear doesn't make us feel good. It might fit badly or be too clingy, too baggy, too revealing or just not be very you. This is no good at all. Sportswear is there to help us be at our best, take on new challenges and enjoy being active. Worrying about what we look like can stop us from enjoying sports as much.

Choose clothes that help you feel confident. Certain styles will feel more comfortable to wear; there might be parts of your body where you want extra support and other places that don't feel good when they're squished under tight fabric. Now, this is great if you're training alone, but sometimes you must wear a team uniform and don't get a choice. Or do you . . . ?

© Katinka Haltvik

The Norwegian Beach Handball team broke the rules at the 2021 European Championships by wearing shorts instead of bikini bottoms. For years athletes had called for change to the strict dress code for women, but were always dismissed. The Norwegian team decided that enough was enough and took action. The crowd cheered loudly when they entered the stadium for the bronze medal match wearing shorts.

Afterwards, each player was fined €150 by the European Handball Federation for disobeying the dress code.

Outrage erupted across the world at the news of their punishment. People criticised the outdated rules, agreeing that women should be allowed to wear what they feel comfortable in. Thanks to the Norwegian team's stand, this rule was changed and women can now wear shorts in beach handball if they choose to.

© Katinka Haltvik

"IT SHOULDN'T BE THE CASE THAT PEOPLE DON'T WANT TO TAKE PART BECAUSE OF THE OUTFIT."

Katinka Haltvik

YOUR VOICE MATTERS

Thanks to the amazing work of athletes and advocates (supporters of a cause), there's been a HUGE shift in the right direction. Rules are changing and sportswear that fits and feels better is being designed specifically for women.

However, there are still some schools and sports clubs with dress codes that should have gone extinct with the dinosaurs. Nobody should force you to wear something that you don't feel comfortable in and, if they try, this is not okay. You know what makes you feel comfortable and confident, and you can have a say in the matter.

Remember, you are not alone in this. If your kit makes you feel uncomfortable then it's probably affecting others too. Together, your voices can make a big difference. Write a letter to a newspaper, start a petition or ask your school or club to change the rules.

LOVE YOUR BODY

Your body is a marvellous machine and you are on a wonderful journey with it. Whilst puberty causes it to change in ways you might not expect, you can still appreciate it for everything it does for you.

Love your strength, your passion and your peculiarities.

Love the things that you've got in common with others and love the things that make you different.

EVERY DAY, **CHOOSE TO LOVE** THE PARTS OF YOURSELF THAT YOU'RE CONTENTED WITH AND KEEP NURTURING ANY FEARFUL BITS – THESE AREAS WILL START TO **BLOSSOM** UNDER **KINDNESS**.

TAKING FEEDBACK LIKE A CHAMP

TAKE A SHOT AT:

Using feedback to help you improve and have more fun. Learning what advice to listen to and how to deal with negative comments (whether they come from others or yourself) helps you create better relationships and nicer environments to play in.

Feedback is a pretty cool tool. It lets you know what you're good at and where you can improve, which in turn helps you enjoy your sport more. Sometimes it can sting a little – maybe because the feedback itself isn't very nice (this happens occasionally), or because you find it tricky to remember where you're doing well. If you look at feedback in a different way, it allows you to get more out of yourself and your sport.

Part of this is making sure the feedback is right for you. Every amazing athlete walks their own path. They face their own set of adversities, rise to their own challenges, discover new talents and find pleasure in what they're doing. Working with these beautiful differences and figuring out how to make the most of them gives us an edge, letting us enjoy the experience more.

SPORT: Tennis

COUNTRY: Great Britain

"Wimbledon was an extremely positive experience. I learnt so much about my game, and what it takes to perform at the top."

EMMA RADUCANU

In 2021, rising tennis star Emma Raducanu, MBE, did something very brave: she pulled out of the fourth round at Wimbledon. Getting this far was a big deal. She was given a wild card – a special invitation for players who haven't made the cut through their world ranking – and she had an incredible run, winning match after match.

This streak came to an end when she experienced breathing difficulties in her fourth-round match and she retired. Knowing when to step away is hard, especially when the cameras are clicking and the home crowd is cheering. Her decision received praise in the media, but it attracted lots of criticism too. Some commentators accused her of not being able to handle the pressure of a major tournament and said she wasn't strong enough.

Two months later, at the US Open, Emma won her first Grand Slam without losing a single set. She takes a special place in sports history because she is the first qualifier – of any gender – to win a Grand Slam title.

LISTEN TO THE PEOPLE WHO MATTER

What a comeback queen! After Wimbledon, the news was full of Emma's epic performance and her shock exit. Overnight everybody became an expert, weighing in on why they thought she withdrew and what she should do. Choosing to listen to the important feedback – from her body and her coaching team – Emma cut through the criticism to deliver extraordinary results.

You might have spotted the trouble with feedback: we can't always control what other people share with us or how they do it. It feels horrible when we're on the receiving end of the negative stuff and it can claw into our confidence – if we let it.

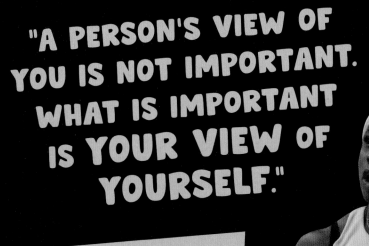

"A PERSON'S VIEW OF YOU IS NOT IMPORTANT. WHAT IS IMPORTANT IS YOUR VIEW OF YOURSELF."

Shelly-Ann Fraser-Pryce

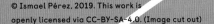

HANDLING CRITICISM LIKE A PRO

Feedback comes in two flavours: the helpful and the hurtful. There is a handy trick to suss out which is which, an ultra-important question you can ask coaches, teammates or whoever else is doling it out:

"HOW WILL THIS HELP ME GET BETTER?"

The whole point of feedback is to help you improve. It's there to celebrate the wins and get you through the gnarly, frustrating patches in between.

When you receive feedback that isn't going to help you improve, you don't have to take it on. Not all feedback comes from a kind place. However, unhelpful feedback doesn't always mean someone is trying to be hurtful. Sometimes an honest conversation can help clear up any misunderstandings.

IT'S NOT PERSONAL

Once we've left unhelpful criticism at the door, we can concentrate on the useful feedback. Even though it can feel totally rubbish to hear where we're going wrong, especially if we're working really hard, try not to take constructive criticism personally.

Remember: it's not about you, it is just an observation of how you're doing at this particular moment.

DRAW A LINE UNDER IT

Write down some critical feedback you have been given. Your sporting efforts and you as a person are two very different things and should never be mixed up, so draw a nice, thick line between you and that criticism. Underneath the line, jot down the ways this information can help you get better.

We don't just get feedback on the sports pitch. It gets dished out by all kinds of people, from coding classes to clarinet practice, and this activity works for any kind of feedback.

TEAM TALK

There is a BIG difference between helpful and hurtful criticism: one is given to help you get better; the other is designed to throw you off your game. Hurtful criticism is never okay and it's never your fault. If you ever experience this, don't be afraid to speak about it to a trusted adult. Keeping your feelings bottled inside can make you feel very alone. We are always stronger together, so sharing it with your support team spreads the load and they can help you figure out what to do.

THE THREE STEPS OF FEEDBACK

Feedback can be given to ourselves as well as taken from other people. Breaking it down into three stages gives us the fullest picture of what is going on. When we have a clearer idea of where we are, it helps us decide what to do next.

STEP 1

WHAT WENT WELL?

The first rule of feedback is to focus on the positives. Appreciate all the things you've aced, and celebrate every solid save, stride or shot. Even if you lose big, there will still be good moments, where glimmers of talent or teamwork shine through. Knowing what's working well is just as important as knowing what isn't, so you can make these areas even stronger.

STEP 2

WHERE CAN I IMPROVE?

It's useful to reflect on the awesome stuff but we need to know where we can get better. This means looking at areas that aren't going so well; the challenges, weak spots and mistakes made.

STEP 3

HOW DO I MAKE THIS HAPPEN?

Action! Knowing you're doing well (or not so well!) is great, but you're only going to improve if you do something about it. Based on this information, what can you do differently next time? And what strengths can you keep making stronger?

THE THREE STEPS OF FEEDBACK

Now it's your turn. After your next practice session or competition answer these three questions:

1 What went well?

2 Where can I improve?

3 How do I make this happen?

Remember, feedback is a precious gift and should always be given with care and respect. When we look at improvement areas, it can be easy to get sucked into the trap of being a bit too self-critical. Putting ourselves down and finding fault with every tiny mistake is a miserable place to be. Even worse, it doesn't help us improve!

Stuffing up sometimes stings and exploring our weaknesses can be draining. We feel these emotions for a reason and it is 100% okay to feel rubbish when things don't go to plan. However, we need to make sure that we don't dwell on these emotions for too long.

I KNOW THIS ISN'T EASY, BUT I DO KNOW THAT IT'S POSSIBLE.

MY STORY

At the European Championships, my first international competition, I took my position on the line as the clock began to count down. I pulled my bow back, took aim, and . . . panicked! My knees knocked, my toes trembled and my fingers fumbled, which, when you're aiming at a target 70 metres away, is not good. My arrows flew everywhere (sadly, not the middle of the target) and that was it.

GAME OVER!

I was gutted. This was my big chance and I'd just blown it. A whopping big wave of emotions hit me – heartache, frustration and so much disappointment – and that was okay! Doing well mattered to me, and I let myself feel those feelings. That evening, I put them to good use, jumping into major learn-from-it mode, and got ready to make some serious improvements. I looked at my performance and asked myself: what could I do better? The big, glaring fact of the matter was that I needed to learn how to handle pressure better – and I did!

A year later I went to the World Championships where I broke eight world records in a week and came away with two gold medals! I'm thankful for this experience because it taught me how much we can learn from the rough patches.

A good trick is to pretend you're giving feedback
to a friend: think about the way you'd explain things to
them without hurting their feelings. If you're finding it
difficult to manage your emotions, try writing about them.
Putting those thoughts onto paper makes them
easier to make sense of.

72

STAY CURIOUS

A shortcut to success? There aren't many of them about, so when we find one
it's a good idea to grab hold of it with both hands. Any experience – whether
good, bad or somewhere in between – gives us important takeaways that
propel us in the right direction. So keep listening, keep learning and stay
curious. Asking the right questions helps us get to the right answers,
and the most important question of all is:

HOW WILL THIS HELP ME GET BETTER?

A FAILURE ISN'T A FAILURE IF IT PREPARES YOU FOR SUCCESS TOMORROW.

Two-time **gold medallist** in bobsled events at the World Championships (2013 and 2021)

One of the few athletes to have competed at both the **Summer** and **Winter Olympics** (2008, 2012 and 2014)

Two-time **gold medallist** in 60m hurdles at the World Indoor Championship (2008 and 2010)

Gold medallist in 100m hurdles at the World Athletics Final (2008)

Lolo Jones, American hurdler and bobsledder

SCHOOL OR SPORT? WHY NOT BOTH?

TAKE A SHOT AT:

Balancing sport with other demands, like school and your social life. We really can have it all, and you'll discover that, when you take part in sport, you're creating an amazing blueprint for success in other areas of your life.

As you grow older, sport can get shuffled down the priority list, as adults start to mutter about exams and other Very Important Responsibilities. Sometimes it's hard to figure out how to squeeze sport and other hobbies in. We're going to start by busting a thumping, big myth . . .

"YOU NEED TO CONCENTRATE ON YOUR EDUCATION BECAUSE IT WILL HELP YOU SUCCEED IN LIFE. SPORT IS JUST A DISTRACTION."

UH OH!

This kind of outdated thinking belongs in the bin. Education opens the door to limitless possibilities – that part is true – but the bit about sport not helping you? **This is so far off the mark!**

Research has shown that 94% of women in top-level jobs in the USA played competitive sport when they were younger. We're not talking about elite athletes here, by the way, but those who participated in regular sporting activities. It doesn't stop there: on average, women who played sport get paid 7% more than those who didn't.

Sport lays some incredible foundations, helping to create leaders of the future. The research shows that the skills learned on the playing field are highly valued off it. I know we're thinking ahead here but, wherever you end up, the sports you are practising now are creating exciting opportunities for your future.

SPORTY SUPER SKILLS

The best teacher I ever had was sport. It helped me hone so many useful skills. I learned how to work in a team and communicate better. It taught me about taking responsibility for my actions, how to thrive in competition and how to problem-solve. I became more confident, and I discovered that when I thought I'd reached my limit I could always dig a little deeper and push a little further.

It also gave me a space where I could shoot arrows and forget about the serious stuff for a little while. Pressure to be the best you can be, get good grades and make lots of friends is piled on by teachers, parents, peers, the media and even yourself. Sometimes it feels a bit much.

We all need time out to do something we enjoy: it's like pressing a reset button that clears your mind, leaving you more refreshed and ready to go.

The amazing new skills I picked up had a very unexpected side effect. They helped me deliver better results in school. Don't just take my word for it. Scientific studies have shown that athletes perform better in school.

YES, THAT'S RIGHT, EXERCISE ACTUALLY HELPS US PASS EXAMS!

So, whilst you're doing your thing on the pitch, in the pool or at the park, you're also getting:

✓ **IMPROVED BRAIN FUNCTION,** MAKING IT EASIER TO LEARN NEW THINGS

✓ GREATER ABILITY TO **CONCENTRATE**

✓ **IMPROVED MEMORY**

✓ **REDUCED** EXAM OR OTHER SCHOOL **PRESSURES**

✓ **MORE ENERGY** TO KEEP YOU GOING FOR LONGER

✓ **BETTER GRADES!**

Not everybody knows this! You can help to spread the word, letting your support team know that sport helps us dream bigger and achieve better – and that you need their help to get this right.

MY STORY

Two years after I started archery, I was on the brink of making the national team. I was practising three times a week and spent most of my weekends zipping around the country to competitions. One day my mum gave me a choice.

"You can pick your sport or your social life."

"We will support whatever decision you make but if you choose archery, it comes first."

Sadly, school wasn't up for discussion!

I chose sport. My friends were (and still are) very important to me, but I knew that archery could lead me on an amazing adventure if I was brave enough to keep going. It also unlocked a new friendship group who had the same interest as me.

I squeezed archery practice around many social activities, but some days I felt a little left out hearing about fun trips and sleepovers I couldn't go to. Because I made this choice myself it made missing out on them a little easier. It helped to remind myself of the brilliant time I'd had – even if my results weren't particularly good – and I found other ways to make time for my friends. When I got to compete on home soil in London 2012 they were cheering in the crowd.

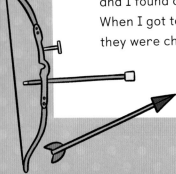

THE BALANCING ACT

Time to get real: these benefits are great, but the truth is that life gets messy when you have lots of different things to focus on. Cramming in sport, school, family time, a social life and all the other activities stacked on your plate can leave you feeling spread too thinly. Striking a balance between these activities makes a hectic timetable much easier to manage.

Balancing sport with school doesn't mean that we split our time into equal portions, with a little bit of sport here, a little bit of school there and some free time for fun if we can squish it in. Some things are more important (or take longer) than others, so we need to make sure we put the right amount of time in the right places.

DID YOU KNOW?
The majority of Olympians don't focus on training full time.
A whacking 68% of athletes have careers outside their sports:
they are lawyers, students, engineers, prison officers,
hairdressers, doctors, teachers, firefighters, coaches,
social media managers and more!

"You must work really hard to fulfil your dream. I had to put in three times the effort of a French student: between learning the language, the university courses and the sport. I lived my dream when the crowd cried out my name."

SPORT: Cycling

COUNTRY: Afghanistan

MASOMAH ALI ZADA

When Masomah Ali Zada was born, girls were not allowed to ride bikes in Afghanistan. It was a dangerous place, so her family fled to Iran as refugees, where her father taught her how to cycle. Riding gave her an incredible sense of freedom and she absolutely loved it.

When her family returned to Afghanistan, she joined the national team. The law had changed, but many people still thought that cycling was not for girls and one day a man in a car knocked her off her bike on purpose.

In 2017 she became a refugee in France. Her sporting goals were supported there and she studied civil engineering at university. Masomah made herself two promises: no matter how tired she was she would make her 8am classes, and no matter how busy she was she would exercise. She was determined to be successful at both – and she was!

As a refugee, Masomah was not allowed to represent her country at the Tokyo 2020 Games. Instead, she competed as part of the Refugee Team. In 2023, she graduated from university and signed up for a Master's degree.

GETTING THE BALANCE RIGHT

Even in the most trying circumstances it is possible to balance more than one big priority!
Just follow these steps . . .

UNDERSTAND YOUR PRIORITIES

STEP 1

If you're passionate about your sport (or sports!) then you will always find a way to turn up and play. Think about all the different things you do, what you really enjoy and what you'd like to achieve both in and outside of sport.

DIVIDE YOUR TIME

STEP 2

Once you know what your priorities are, you need to decide how much time to spend on each one. Think about how you can use your time wisely. Using a calendar or a diary is a great way to keep on top of all the things that need doing and any big milestones that you've got coming up.

FLEX THE PLAN

STEP 3

Situations change and so must we: sometimes something Big and Important crops up that needs your attention right away. Keep checking in with Steps 1 and 2 to make sure your priorities are set properly and shuffle your schedule around if you need to.

WORKING SMARTER NOT HARDER

There will be days when your to-do list gets so long you can't find the bottom of it. If things are rocketing out of control, take a deep breath and get the urgent stuff out of the way first. Stretching ourselves is good and we can manage busy times in short bursts, but if we try to juggle too many things all the time we overstretch ourselves and – **SPLAT** – our energy levels take a nosedive.

> HIGH PERFORMANCE SPORTS AND TRAINING IS HARD, SO YOU HAVE TO ENJOY IT EVERY DAY. AND IF THAT SPORT IS COMPETITIVE, YOU ENJOY IT EVEN MORE BECAUSE IT REALLY IS A DISPLAY OF EVERY HOUR OF WORK YOU HAVE DEVOTED TO PRACTISING IT.

Ruth Beitia

If you're overdoing it, you will never be able to show up at your very best, so you need to learn how to do more with less. This might be learning how to speed up without cutting corners or saying, "No!" to certain things. This can be hard, especially if it feels like you're letting somebody else down. Think of it as a kindness to yourself and to others because if you're not able to give 100% to something then you aren't helping anybody.

SCHOOL, SPORT . . . AND SOCIAL?

Life isn't meant to burst at the seams with only school and sport. No matter how busy you are, spending time with friends and family helps you build important connections and recharge your batteries – not to mention that it's a whole lot of fun!

Balance is about splitting your time up in the best way for you. Your aspirations in sport (or any of your other activities) change what this balance looks like and how much time you spend in each area.

If you are finding it tricky to know what to prioritise, it might be helpful to look at how to use your passions as a guiding star (page 18).

I'VE GOT EPIC PLANS FOR MY SPORT

If you want your sport to take you places then you have to dial up the effort to get better at it. Sacrifices will have to be made and, yes, there will be times when you feel you are missing out. We may feel resentful but it helps to think about it in a different way: focus on the opportunities you gain through sport, the fun you're having and the progress you're making.

M T W T F S S

Choosing sport does not mean spending 100% of your time on it outside of school. Rest is an essential part of any athlete's training schedule because it stops us from burning out, so building social activities into your weekly schedule is also super important.

FOR ME
SPORT IS ALL
ABOUT THE FUN FACTOR

This is an AWESOME goal too!
Your balance will be lighter on sport and
heavier in other areas. This doesn't mean that
sacrifices won't crop up – life has a habit of throwing
calendar collisions at us, and the decisions we make
here are important and meaningful.

TEAM TALK

Remember, **YOU** sit right at the heart
of this balancing act. If you don't look after
yourself then it's going to be impossible to get the best
results. When you're rushing from one activity to the next
it's easy to forget to rest or care for yourself. Your health
and wellbeing is the biggest priority on your list,
so make sure you have enough time
to sleep, eat well and relax.

SUPER SQUAD

The wonderful thing about friends is they care about the stuff you care about (at least the good ones do!). If you have big dreams, then share them with your pals. Tell them about your sport and why it's important to you and let them know that they matter to you as well. Good friends will support you and they might even want to join in!

Another great activity for the super squad is to think of some things you can do together. You might want to play a game of pickleball in the park, do disc golf as a group or try something you've never done before.

© Vera Prokhorova, Shutterstock, 2024

YOU CAN HAVE IT ALL

Phewf! Organising and prioritising your life isn't glamorous (especially if you're as messy as me!), but it helps you to enjoy your time to the fullest and reach your incredible potential. At points you might not know how to fit everything in, especially if you're getting pressure to focus on your schoolwork, sport, family, community, music or any other activities. Be guided by the reason you play sport, whether it's aiming for huge targets, smaller stepping stones, new experiences or having a great time!

THIS IS YOUR CHOICE AND WHATEVER YOU CHOOSE, YOU CAN ENJOY – AND BE BRILLIANT – AT MORE THAN ONE THING.

MY ADVICE TO ANYONE UNSURE ABOUT PLAYING COMPETITIVE SPORT IS TO GIVE IT A GO.

First hijabi Muslim woman to play and score in the **Women's Premiership**

Winner of the Sunday Times Grassroots Sportswoman of the Year award (2020)

Founder of **Studs in the Mud**, an initiative aimed at providing rugby equipment to grassroots clubs

RICOH
imagine. change.

YES IT MAY BE CHALLENGING BUT . . . I CAN SAY ALL THE JUGGLING IS WORTH IT.

Zainab Alema, British-Ghanaian rugby player

© Tim Anger

P.10

JUNKO TABEI

SPORT: Mountaineering

COUNTRY: Japan

AWESOME ACHIEVEMENT:
First woman to climb Mount Everest.

TRIVIA: Led clean-ups to clear the rubbish left on mountains in Japan and the Himalayas.

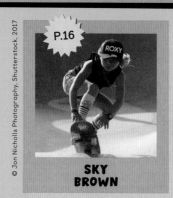

P.16

SKY BROWN

SPORT: Skateboarding

COUNTRY: UK

AWESOME ACHIEVEMENT:
Two-time bronze medallist, winning her first medal at the Tokyo 2020 Olympics aged 13.

TRIVIA: Youngest person to represent the UK at the Summer Olympics.

P.20

BEATRICE 'BEBE' VIO

SPORT: Fencing

COUNTRY: Italy

AWESOME ACHIEVEMENT:
Six Paralympic medals: two gold, one silver and three bronze. She is the first quadruple amputee to win a medal in fencing.

TRIVIA: Founded a charity to give sports opportunities to disabled children.

P.25

MO'NE DAVIS

SPORT: Baseball and Softball

COUNTRY: USA

AWESOME ACHIEVEMENT:
First girl to pitch a shutout in the history of the Little League World Series.

TRIVIA: Enjoys playing basketball.

P.28

ALICE MILLIAT

SPORT: Rowing

COUNTRY: France

AWESOME ACHIEVEMENT:
Organised the first international female athletic competitions and got more women's events added to the Olympics.

TRIVIA: Gifted at languages and worked as a translator.

P.29

MARY EARPS, MBE

SPORT: Football

COUNTRY: England

AWESOME ACHIEVEMENT:
Winner of the Golden Glove award for best goalkeeper at the 2023 FIFA Women's World Cup and part of the winning team at the Euros 2022.

TRIVIA: Black belt in judo.

P.38

KULSOOM ABDULLAH

SPORT: Weightlifting

COUNTRY: Pakistan/USA

AWESOME ACHIEVEMENT:
First woman to compete in weightlifting wearing a hijab with arms and legs covered, following her campaign to change the rules.

TRIVIA: Has a PhD in electrical and computer engineering.

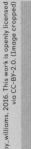

P.34

HAYLEY WICKENHEISER

SPORT: Ice Hockey

COUNTRY: Canada

AWESOME ACHIEVEMENT:
Four-time Olympic gold medallist. Also played softball at the 2000 Olympic Games.

TRIVIA: Trained as a doctor when she retired from sport.

P.41

BETHANY HAMILTON

SPORT: Surfing

COUNTRY: USA

AWESOME ACHIEVEMENT:
Shark-bite survivor and winner of the Pipeline Women's Pro.

TRIVIA: Loves spending time at the beach and cooking.

P.44

JASMIN PARIS, MBE

SPORT: Ultra Endurance Running

COUNTRY: UK

AWESOME ACHIEVEMENT:
Winner of the 268-mile Winter Spine Race in 2019 and first female finisher of the Barkley Marathons.

TRIVIA: Works as a vet, and likes to paint, bake and read.

P.58

KATINKA HALTVIK

SPORT: Beach Handball

COUNTRY: Norway

AWESOME ACHIEVEMENT:
Former team captain and advocate for appropriate sports clothing.

TRIVIA: Balanced a career in law while competing.

P.50

FU YUANHUI

SPORT: Swimming

COUNTRY: China

AWESOME ACHIEVEMENT:
Bronze medallist at Rio 2016 Olympic Games.

TRIVIA: Started swimming to improve her asthma.

CHARLOTTE HENSHAW, MBE

P.57

SPORT: Swimming and canoe

COUNTRY: UK

AWESOME ACHIEVEMENT:
Five Paralympic medals (three golds, a silver and a bronze) in two different sports.

TRIVIA: Can be found watching musicals when not training.

SERENA WILLIAMS

P.61

SPORT: Tennis

COUNTRY: USA

AWESOME ACHIEVEMENT:
23 Grand Slam singles wins and four Olympic gold medals.

TRIVIA: Favourite author is poet and civil rights activist, Maya Angelou.

EMMA RADUCANU, MBE

P.64

SPORT: Tennis

COUNTRY: UK

AWESOME ACHIEVEMENT:
First qualifier of any gender to win a Grand Slam title.

TRIVIA: Enjoys watching Formula One and playing the board game mahjong.

RUTH BEITIA

P.83

SPORT: High Jump

COUNTRY: Spain

AWESOME ACHIEVEMENT:
Won Olympic gold in Rio 2016, becoming the oldest gold medallist in any jumping event.

TRIVIA: Whilst competing at the top level, she also worked as a politician.

ZAINAB ALEMA

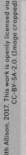

P.89

SPORT: Rugby

COUNTRY: UK

AWESOME ACHIEVEMENT:
Winner of the Sunday Times Grassroots Sportswoman of the Year award 2020.

TRIVIA: Worked as a neonatal nurse and helped save lives during the COVID-19 pandemic.

LYDIA KO

P.101

SPORT: Golf

COUNTRY: New Zealand

AWESOME ACHIEVEMENT:
The youngest player to reach world number one ranking, winner of over 20 LPGA titles and Olympic gold medallist from Paris 2024.

TRIVIA: Enjoys binge-watching Netflix and cooking.

50:00

P.103

RACHAEL BLACKMORE, MBE

SPORT: Horse Racing

COUNTRY: Ireland

AWESOME ACHIEVEMENT:
First female jockey to win the Grand National and the Cheltenham Gold Cup.

TRIVIA: Likes eating ice cream.

P.108

CAITLIN CLARK

SPORT: Basketball

COUNTRY: USA

AWESOME ACHIEVEMENT:
Most all-time points scored by a college player – male or female.

TRIVIA: Plays video games and golf in her spare time.

P.111

ASHLEY FIOLEK

SPORT: Motocross

COUNTRY: USA

AWESOME ACHIEVEMENT:
First deaf professional motocross racer and four-time national champion.

TRIVIA: Works as a stunt actor and has a dog called Bambi.

93

P.115

SIMONE BILES

SPORT: Gymnastics

COUNTRY: USA

AWESOME ACHIEVEMENT:
Seven Olympic gold medals and twenty-three (!) time world champion.

TRIVIA: Loves Italian food and shopping.

P.118

LEAH WILLIAMSON, OBE

SPORT: Football

COUNTRY: England

AWESOME ACHIEVEMENT:
Captained England women's football team with historic win at the Euros 2022.

TRIVIA: Can do back-flips and enjoys Sudoku puzzles.

P.122

MALAIKA MIHAMBO

SPORT: Long Jump

COUNTRY: Germany

AWESOME ACHIEVEMENT:
Olympic gold and silver medallist and two-time world champion.

TRIVIA: Plays the piano and does yoga in her spare time.

P.126

ANAÏS BESCOND

SPORT: Biathlon

COUNTRY: France

AWESOME ACHIEVEMENT:
Won two individual Olympic bronze medals and a gold medal in the mixed relay event.

TRIVIA: Serves as a sergeant in the French armed forces.

P.127

MITHALI RAJ

SPORT: Cricket

COUNTRY: India

AWESOME ACHIEVEMENT:
National team captain for 18 years and regarded as one of the greatest cricketers ever.

TRIVIA: Wanted to be a classical dancer when she was growing up.

P.130

PERES JEPCHIRCHIR

SPORT: Long-distance Running

COUNTRY: Kenya

AWESOME ACHIEVEMENT:
First athlete to win an Olympic gold and the New York City Marathon in the same year.

TRIVIA: Helped design a running shoe with Adidas.

94

P.131

MARY KEITANY

SPORT: Marathon Runner

COUNTRY: Kenya

AWESOME ACHIEVEMENT:
World-record-holder and seven-time marathon winner.

TRIVIA: Favourite race is the London Marathon because of the spectators cheering the runners on.

P.135

MEGAN RAPINOE

SPORT: Football

COUNTRY: USA

AWESOME ACHIEVEMENT:
Winner of the Best FIFA Women's Player award in 2019, two-time World Cup winner and Olympic gold medallist.

TRIVIA: Has a twin sister who also plays football.

P.136

GISELA PULIDO

SPORT: Kitesurfing

COUNTRY: Spain

AWESOME ACHIEVEMENT:
World champion aged 10; beat adults to claim the title.

TRIVIA: Inspired to try kitesurfing after watching her dad doing it.

P.137

SARAH MENEZES

SPORT: Judo

COUNTRY: Brazil

AWESOME ACHIEVEMENT:
First Brazilian woman to win a Olympic gold medal in judo and head coach of national judo team.

TRIVIA: Her parents disapproved of her doing judo, so she had to practise in secret.

P.139

DINA ASHER-SMITH

SPORT: Sprinter

COUNTRY: UK

AWESOME ACHIEVEMENT:
Fastest British woman on record, Olympic silver medallist and world champion.

TRIVIA: Did street jazz dancing when she was younger.

P.141

RONDA ROUSEY

SPORT: Wrestling and Judo

COUNTRY: USA

AWESOME ACHIEVEMENT:
Bronze Olympic medallist in judo and champion professional wrestler.

TRIVIA: Runs an eco-farm.

P.148

LISA BLAIR

SPORT: Sailing

COUNTRY: Australia

AWESOME ACHIEVEMENT:
Five-time world record holder and fastest person to sail around Antarctica solo.

TRIVIA: Decorated her yacht with colourful climate action messages from people around the world.

P.150

JESSICA ENNIS-HILL, DBE

SPORT: Heptathlon

COUNTRY: UK

AWESOME ACHIEVEMENT:
Olympic gold medallist and three-time world champion.

TRIVIA: Favourite heptathlon event is the hurdles.

P.159

LINDSEY COLE

SPORT: Adventuring

COUNTRY: UK

AWESOME ACHIEVEMENT:
Environmental activist who swims as a mermaid to raise awareness of pollution in our waterways.

TRIVIA: Roller-skated from Bristol to Paris in 2013, having never skated before.

NATALIA PARTYKA

SPORT: Table Tennis

COUNTRY: Poland

AWESOME ACHIEVEMENT:
Six-time Paralympic gold medallist and four-time Olympian.

TRIVIA: Loves relaxing at the beach during her time off.

P.156

MIA HAMM

SPORT: Football

COUNTRY: USA

AWESOME ACHIEVEMENT:
Two-time Olympic gold medallist; considered one of the world's best footballers.

TRIVIA: Enjoys playing golf and watching basketball.

P.164

ZAHRA LARI

SPORT: Figure Skating

COUNTRY: United Arab Emirates

AWESOME ACHIEVEMENT:
First figure skater from the Middle East to compete internationally.

TRIVIA: Favourite colour is purple.

P.162

P.153

TRICIA DOWNING

SPORT: Ironman

COUNTRY: USA

AWESOME ACHIEVEMENT:
The first female paraplegic athlete to complete an Ironman triathlon.

TRIVIA: Also represented her country in rowing and shooting.

WHAT SPORT SHOULD I CHOOSE?

....

I BELIEVE IN YOU

TAKE A SHOT AT:

Believing in yourself, staying positive when things get tough, and saying, "Yes" to new opportunities. Confidence is a must-have skill that touches every aspect of our lives: it picks us up through difficult times and keeps us going through the good times.

"YOU NEED TO BE MORE CONFIDENT!"

I'm willing to bet that someone, somewhere, has said this to you. When we're feeling a little out of our depth (trying a new skill, perhaps?), it seems to be the first piece of advice that gets handed out.

It might be meant well, but on a scale of one to absolutely useless, it sits somewhere between completely pointless and outrageously unhelpful.

MY STORY

For as long as I can remember, I was told that I needed to be more confident. It came from my parents, teachers and coaches – but none of them showed me how. It was as if by telling me to be more confident I'd somehow miraculously develop it! My confidence continued to fluctuate – sometimes it was sky high but other times it dipped so low that I worried I'd never amount to anything.

This shaky relationship with confidence came crashing to the ground at the Paralympic Games in Beijing 2008. After getting off to a world-record-breaking start, I made it through to the semi-finals. Only two matches separated me from the gold medal I desperately wanted to win. The night before those two matches I had a bit of a mental meltdown.

It started with one thought: *I want this so badly, but what if I can't pull it off tomorrow?*

This was quickly followed by another. *What if my best isn't good enough?*

I slipped into a negative spiral. *What if I let myself down? What if I let everybody back home down?*

I found myself sinking under this pile of negative thoughts until I believed my dream of becoming Paralympic champion was impossible. Luckily I opened a good luck message from the guy who worked on my equipment: "You can shoot scores in your sleep that your competitors can only ever dream about."

The fact that somebody else believed in me gave me the boost I needed, and I went to bed feeling much better. The next day I shot my socks off, storming through my matches with two very convincing wins.

Bursting with pride, I stood on top of the podium with a beautiful gold medal around my neck. Paralympic champion, a dream come true! As the national anthem played, I was struck by this flashing realisation: if I'd gone out there thinking I was going to lose then I would have done. I managed to turn it around at the very last moment, but I learned something very important – we can think ourselves into failure.

I couldn't leave it to chance next time. If I wanted to keep winning medals (and I *really* did!), I had to believe in myself more. Those rather unhelpful adults were right: I did need to be more confident and now I was determined to learn all about it. I wanted to know what confidence was and how I could gain it.

© Danielle Brown

BELIEVING IN YOURSELF

Confidence is believing in your ability. This is super simple to describe, but not always easy to pull off in practice. We all get dips in performance and it can really knock our self-esteem.

New Zealand golfer Lydia Ko was unstoppable. World number one at just 17, she hung onto the top spot for a staggering 85 weeks, delivering one brilliant performance after another.

In 2018 she ran into a dry spell. Putting a lot of pressure on herself to keep winning, she lost confidence in her swing and her ranking dropped quickly. For three years she struggled to get back to winning form but, bit by bit, she built her confidence back up and made an epic comeback in 2021, winning an LPGA Tour event and a bronze medal at Tokyo 2020, then a gold at Paris 2024!

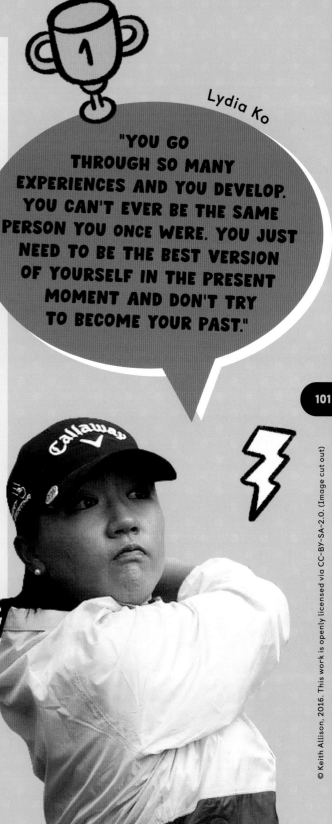

Lydia Ko

"YOU GO THROUGH SO MANY EXPERIENCES AND YOU DEVELOP. YOU CAN'T EVER BE THE SAME PERSON YOU ONCE WERE. YOU JUST NEED TO BE THE BEST VERSION OF YOURSELF IN THE PRESENT MOMENT AND DON'T TRY TO BECOME YOUR PAST."

101

CONFIDENCE GOES UP AND DOWN

It is totally normal for our confidence to slump from time to time and to doubt ourselves at critical moments. This stops us from being at our best – but we can grow our confidence and control the nasty, niggly thoughts that try to put us off. Being confident isn't about being dead certain of yourself all the time. You won't sidestep every failure like a dodgeball world champ, but confidence will encourage you to try again if you do fail. It lets you step up to new opportunities and experiences, rather than avoiding them.

TEAM TALK

Some people believe that confidence is either something you have or something you don't. Wrong! Confidence is like a muscle: we've all got some and it gets stronger when you work it out. Just like a muscle, it can get tired and needs to be looked after to get back to full strength.

DID YOU KNOW?

You can feel confident in some areas of your life and not in others. You might be unfazed when speaking to a room full of people but get the jitters when it's your turn to bat in a cricket match. Not to worry. When we learn how to build confidence, it spills over into all parts of our lives.

I LOVE SPORT, SO I KNOW ITS VALUE – TO HELP CONFIDENCE, SELF-BELIEF, TEAM-BUILDING,

Two-time **winner** of the Champion Hurdle at Cheltenham Festival (2021 and 2022)

First female jockey to win the **Grand National** (2021)

THERE'S LOADS OF DIFFERENT SKILLS THAT CAN BE TRANSFERABLE.

Rachael Blackmore MBE, Irish jockey

CHANGE YOUR DEFINITION OF SUCCESS

Confidence is the most valuable gift you can ever give yourself and there are some brilliant techniques to help you build it.

LEARN FROM FAILURE

This is a big part of getting better at anything and it helps to think of failure as an experience that teaches us how to improve. But – and it's a tremendously big but – it's no good changing how we see failure if we don't also change the way we see success.

© Neiron Photo. Shutterstock. 2017

CELEBRATE THE MINI MILESTONES.

These small achievements will help us to create much bigger successes in the future. Each micro success is like a brick. It might not feel like much at the time, but when you collect enough of them you begin to build something spectacular. Sometimes we have bad days, but if you recover faster than you've managed before, you've made progress – and this is an achievement.

LOOK AT SUCCESS DIFFERENTLY.

It isn't just the big wins. If we spent all our time chasing these kinds of achievements, we'd miss some pretty epic stuff. It could be as simple as turning up to training each week, having a good time at practice sessions or not quitting after a tough one, or the technique you've been working on finally clicking into place. Even small steps take us in the right direction.

THE ACHIEVEMENT VAULT

Make a list of all your achievements, from the very big to the very small. They don't just have to be in sport – confidence is something we want in all areas of our life, after all.

Play around with this if you don't fancy writing the world's longest list. You could add pictures or photos, or even turn it into a family activity where you all share what you've achieved each day. This is a good idea if you find it difficult to think of all the amazing things you've accomplished because others often see things that we can't.

If you feel nervous about something or your confidence is shuddering like a diving board after take-off, then open your vault. All these remarkable successes teach you that you can overcome anything because you've dealt with tricky situations before and come through it.

MY ACHIEVEMENT VAULT

1		✓
2		✓
3		✓

ADD TO YOUR ACHIEVEMENT VAULT EVERY
TIME YOU ACHIEVE SOMETHING NEW.
YOUR CONFIDENCE WILL KEEP GROWING
AS YOU COLLECT MORE AMAZING WINS.

"I've worked really hard to be in this moment. And that's where my confidence comes from."

108

SPORT: Basketball

COUNTRY: USA

AWESOME ATHLETE

CAITLIN CLARK

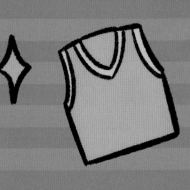

Women's basketball games are selling out fast as huge crowds flock to watch Caitlin Clark. She's a scoring sensation, leading teams to victory with unbelievably precise shooting when it counts.

When Caitlin was eight she wrote her goal on a piece of paper: "I want to play in the WNBA." Her parents couldn't find a girls' basketball team so they signed her up to a boys' league and she was soon the best player on the court. She progressed fast and smashed the record as the highest scorer in college basketball history, male or female. When she graduated she achieved her dream – she was the first pick for the WNBA, signed by pro team Indiana Fever.

Her exceptional skill has changed the game and fans travel across the world to watch her play.

Caitlin continues to rise to the occasion, delivering one stunning performance after another. She scores 45.5% of the shots she takes, but she also stays positive when she misses. Caitlin draws confidence from knowing that she has worked hard and deserves her place on the team.

THE POWER OF POSITIVITY

Thoughts are a bit like seeds. Negative thoughts spread and grow into unhelpful feelings, like my blip in Beijing, and nibble away at our confidence. But do you know something super cool? Positive thoughts do the same thing in reverse. When we plant positive thoughts, they grow into constructive feelings and behaviours.

Positivity is an important ingredient because it changes how you see the world, even when stuff goes wrong.

It's easier to handle challenges if you see them as a temporary setback rather than an everything's-gone-horribly-wrong-so-I-may-as-well-give-up kind of disaster. Focusing on actions and solutions helps you take control.

You have the power to plant the right thoughts by thinking about positive outcomes. Now, this doesn't magically erase feelings like disappointment, frustration, anger or uncertainty. You will still get these big feelings sometimes – and this is totally okay – but you won't get overwhelmed by them. The comforting words on the next page encourage you to keep your head in the game and to try hard even when it gets tough.

"I believe in my ability."

"I will give it my all today."

"I am stronger than I was yesterday."

My personal fave is:

"You can do this!"

I repeat these words to myself when I'm pulling back my bow, speaking to a packed assembly hall or about to sit in front of my laptop ready to write my next book. I've got them hanging on my wall in bold, bright letters to remind me on those groggy, grey mornings when my brain is a little foggy and forgetful.

Ashley Fiolek

"YOU JUST HAVE TO BE BRAVE ENOUGH TO GO AHEAD AND DO IT. YOU GET BETTER BY DOING IT OVER, AGAIN AND AGAIN."

TEAM TALK

It's normal to have doubts, but if the ball of worry in your stomach doesn't go away then please reach out and talk to somebody. There are lots of people who can help, such as parents, other trusted adults, friends or your GP. Sometimes opening up can really help you understand and manage these feelings better.

ACTIVITY

TAKE THIS QUIZ to help you understand how confident you feel about yourself and identify the areas where you can grow. Remember, this is where you are right now, not where you want to be, so answer these questions honestly and add up how many points you get.

How do you feel about trying a new sport?

QUESTION 1

A) Sign me up! I'm excited and can't wait to start.

B) I feel nervous but I'm willing to give it a go.

C) Not for me, thanks! I like sticking with what I know.

What do you do if a coach or teammate gives you a compliment?

QUESTION 2

A) I say thank you. It feels great to be praised.

B) I am happy, but sometimes I'm not sure what to say.

C) I downplay it because they don't really mean it.

How do you react when you make a mistake?

QUESTION 3

A) I learn from it and move on.

B) I'm disappointed, but consider where I could improve.

C) I get upset with myself and start to doubt my abilities.

How do you usually face a tough patch with training?

QUESTION 4

A) I stay positive and tackle it head-on.

B) I take it one step at a time and ask for help if I need it.

C) I get stressed as I worry it means I'm not good enough.

Can you easily write down all your abilities and strengths?

A) Yes, I have many strengths I'm proud of.

B) I can think of some strengths and abilities.

C) I'd struggle to find many things I'm good at.

How do you react when you're given feedback?

A) I'm glad because I can use it to improve.

B) It stings a little, but I understand that it's helpful.

C) I take it personally and feel discouraged.

When you're playing in a team, how do you normally take part?

A) I'm an active participant and I like to take the lead.

B) I like to contribute, but I'm not always sure where I fit in.

C) I follow the others and let them take charge.

How do you feel about yourself overall?

A) I am confident and happy with who I am.

B) I have ups and downs. Some days I feel more sure of myself than others.

C) I often feel unsure about myself.

TURN OVER TO SEE YOUR RESULTS

ACTIVITY

MOSTLY A

You are super confident! You believe in yourself and are not afraid to take on new challenges. Remember: confidence is like a rechargeable battery. It needs to be topped up sometimes!

You can do this by:
• Trying something new. This helps your comfort zone to grow.
• Helping others who are less confident than you. This lets you build a deeper relationship with your own confidence.

MOSTLY B

Your confidence is growing, but this can change if you experience a setback or new situation. There are lots of ways to handle the moments of doubt.

Have a go at:
• Visualising success. Picture yourself calmly mastering a challenging skill and think about how good it will feel when you achieve it.
• Putting in maximum effort and practising hard. If you've prepared yourself well you will feel ready to turn up and play well.

MOSTLY C

You find it hard to step out of your comfort zone, but you have so many strengths hiding under those doubts.

Why not try:
• Writing a thank you letter to yourself explaining what you like about yourself.
• Making a playlist that makes you feel good about yourself. Play it before you practise sport, or any time you need a boost!

I BELIEVE IN YOU

I know that you have everything it takes to be who you want to be and achieve your goals – both inside sport and out of it. On this amazing journey, never forget to stop and marvel at how far you've come. Celebrate the amazing skills you've learned, the friendships you've built, and the challenges you have overcome. There is no limit to your potential, and more of it shines through every time you choose to ignore that little voice that tries to knock you off course.

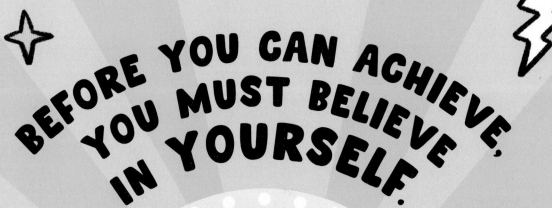

BEFORE YOU CAN ACHIEVE, YOU MUST BELIEVE IN YOURSELF.

Most decorated gymnast in history, with 11 Olympic medals and 30 World Championship medals

Nine-time winner of the US national all-around championship

YOU ARE MORE CAPABLE THAN YOU THINK.

Simone Biles, American gymnast

THE DREAM TEAM

TAKE A SHOT AT:

Creating a team of people who support you, believe in you and want to help you thrive in sport, and beyond.

Sport is best played together. This is pretty obvious if you play netball where the whole team works together in a match, but it's also true for individual sports like taekwondo.

Okay, so a teammate isn't going to leap in and deliver an epic front snap kick on your behalf, but they help you become awesome at your sport nonetheless. Clubmates and coaches are a big part of your sports experience and when you have fun together as a team you achieve so much more.

Your support team is far BIGGER than that inner circle at your club: when you start to look closely, you'll find a whole crowd of people behind you. Your team might include parents, carers, teachers, siblings, cousins, friends or the farmer down the road (a farmer used to let me use one of his fields to practise in!).

This team makes it possible for you to succeed; they make the journey more interesting and facing challenges together breaks them down more easily.

"The more you give to other people, the more you get back and the more successful you become as a team."

ENGLAND V GERMANY
31 JULY 2022
UEFA WOMENS EURO FINAL

SPORT: Football
COUNTRY: England

LEAH WILLIAMSON

AWESOME ATHLETE

Leah Williamson, OBE, began kicking a ball around whilst she waited for her parents to pick her up from gymnastics. Being part of a team was one of the reasons she fell in love with football, but there weren't any local girls' clubs in her area. Lots of boys' teams wouldn't let her play with them, until one finally agreed to give her a chance as long as she kept up with the boys. Leah didn't just keep up: she quickly became the best player on the team and was invited to train at Arsenal's academy when she was nine.

Proving her worth as a defender, Leah was soon playing for the senior squad and made her debut for Arsenal the day after her 17th birthday. In 2022, she was chosen to be England captain at the UEFA Women's Euros because of the example she set on the pitch. In front of over 87,000 spectators, Leah led the Lionesses to a 2-1 victory. Each athlete on the team brought a hunger to win and a different set of strengths, and when they worked together they were unstoppable. Leah encouraged her team to forget the pressure of being in the finals and play from their hearts.

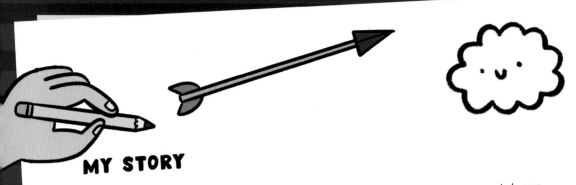

MY STORY

As soon as I finished my last university exam, I jumped in my car and drove straight to an international competition. It was a grey, miserable day, and a big gust of wind blew my arrow off course until . . . whoops! It missed the target completely. My opponent managed a little better. She hit the very outside ring of the target and scored one point, but it was one more than me. She won the gold, and I came away with silver.

I wanted to tell my mum but I knew that she would ask me what went wrong. Sure enough, when I told her the news about my silver medal, it was the first thing she said . . . "I didn't want to ring because I knew you were going to say that, and it's just too much pressure," I finally admitted.

This was one of the best talks I had with my mum about my sport. You see, she was trying her best and she knew that I wouldn't have been happy if she'd sung, "Well done you!" down the phone like she wanted to. I was pretty miffed because my fitness was down after all that revising, and I'd struggled to read the conditions. She was right: a hearty, "Well done" wasn't what I needed at that moment, but neither was, "What went wrong?". This turned into a super healthy conversation about what support was helpful and what was not. We talked about how tough the pressure sometimes felt, and how I needed a safe space to share my worries and process my thoughts. Above all, I needed to feel like somebody else believed in me.

Three years later I represented Great Britain at the London 2012 Paralympic Games and my parents gave me a giant Good Luck card.

On the front were lots of photos of me. Inside, the message read:

"We have watched you grow into the amazing young woman you are today, and we are so proud of you. Just making the team is an incredible achievement – do your best, but most importantly, enjoy the experience."

I pinned it to my bedroom wall in the Olympic Village. Whenever the pressure got a bit too much, I'd look at that card to remind myself that I did archery because I loved it and I deserved to enjoy every second of the Games.

Some of this pressure wasn't caused by my parents at all but by me! I wanted my mum and dad to be proud of me and I worried that if I didn't stay at the top, they'd be disappointed. These big feelings added to the normal pressures of competition. Talking about them and understanding that my parents were proud of me whether I stood on top of the podium or bombed out in the first round really helped. It took some of the pressure off, so I could concentrate on doing what I loved most – shooting my bow.

GETTING THE RIGHT HELP

Being a team player means giving something back too, whether that's maximum effort at practice, words of encouragement to a teammate or listening to feedback. As Leah says, the more you give, the more you get back. So, let's think about your supporters and how you can build the dream team.

"[MY COACH IS] REALLY KIND-HEARTED – ALWAYS LOOKS AT ME AS A PERSON, NOT ONLY AS AN ATHLETE."

Malaika Mihambo

We sometimes slip up on the sports field as we learn to get better, and our support team doesn't always get it right either. Nobody is to blame in these situations: good communication takes a lot of practice. If it goes wrong, then it gives you the opportunity to be honest about what you need so you can get better at this skill together.

"You can do it!"

TEAM TALK

Be brave and talk about your goals, challenges and fears both in sport and outside of it. You might not have the right words to describe some of your feelings or know what you want to achieve (yet!) or what help you need. With practice these conversations become easier and open up a whole new way of thinking.

SUPPORTING THE PERSON, NOT JUST THE ATHLETE

The best supporters understand that sport is a huge part of your life but that you have other interests and abilities too. They see you as an individual and nurture your amazing skills, qualities and brilliant personality quirks.

After an agonising fourth place finish in Rio 2016, long jumper Malaika Mihambo switched to a different coaching team just before Tokyo 2020. She picked the coach who would help her become a better person as well as a better athlete. This proved to be a winning combination – in a nail-biting final she delivered gold on her very last jump.

WHO IS ON MY TEAM?

Remember, a team isn't just made up of the other players in your sports club. It's anybody who helps you with your hobbies, ambitions or education. Have a think about the people currently supporting you:

Who is already on my team?

Have I told them what I'd like to achieve? And what I'm worried about?

Am I getting the right support from them?

What can I say to my team to make sure I get the help I need?

FINDING A PLACE TO BELONG

It can feel scary when you meet a new team for the first time. If the thought of meeting so many new people or trying an activity you've never done before has you feeling worried then ask a friend or sibling to come along with you.

Working on a common goal together and learning to trust each other is a fantastic foundation for lifelong friendships.

Together, we can create a safe space where everybody feels like they belong. This checklist helps you to become a better team player:

MY CHECKLIST

1	Listen to your teammates and coaches carefully, even if you don't agree with them. Their views are important and can help us all grow.	✓
2	You bring some incredible gifts to your team and so do others. They might be different to yours so it's helpful to understand what they are and how they contribute to the team.	✓
3	Be reliable: show up on time and always try your best. Your team are giving their time too so it's only fair to do the same.	✓

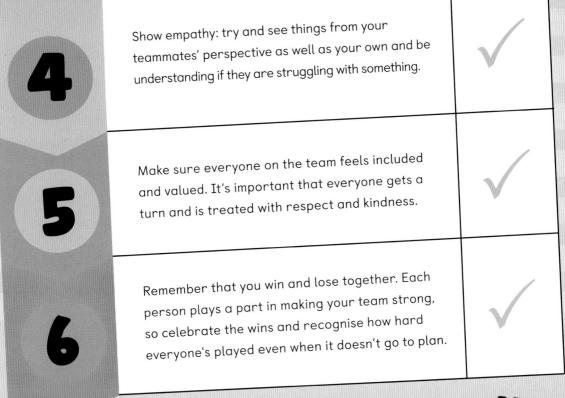

4	Show empathy: try and see things from your teammates' perspective as well as your own and be understanding if they are struggling with something.	✓
5	Make sure everyone on the team feels included and valued. It's important that everyone gets a turn and is treated with respect and kindness.	✓
6	Remember that you win and lose together. Each person plays a part in making your team strong, so celebrate the wins and recognise how hard everyone's played even when it doesn't go to plan.	✓

The beautiful thing about sport is that it brings people with different personalities, skills and backgrounds together. We can't be awesome at EVERYTHING so this combination of winning skills makes the whole team better and lets bright new ideas shine.

CHIEF CHEERLEADER

Now we're going to shine the spotlight on your team with a fun little challenge. You've been given the very important job of Chief Cheerleader and it's your mission to compliment a teammate at every session. Did they do a stunning bounce pass, communicate well or make you feel included?

Choose somebody different each time and don't forget your extended team too! Coaches and family members deserve a bit of cheerleading as well!

BRINGING OTHERS ALONG WITH YOU

You get to choose your interests and your goals, but you do not have to chase them on your own. It's much more fun to share this journey with others and bring them with you. So lean in and ask for help, but make sure you help others too because, together, we can achieve far more than we can on our own.

Brilliant teams aren't built with the best skills and talent, but with kindness, trust and respect. Knowing that your team has your back and trusting them with your sporting aspirations encourages you to give it your all.

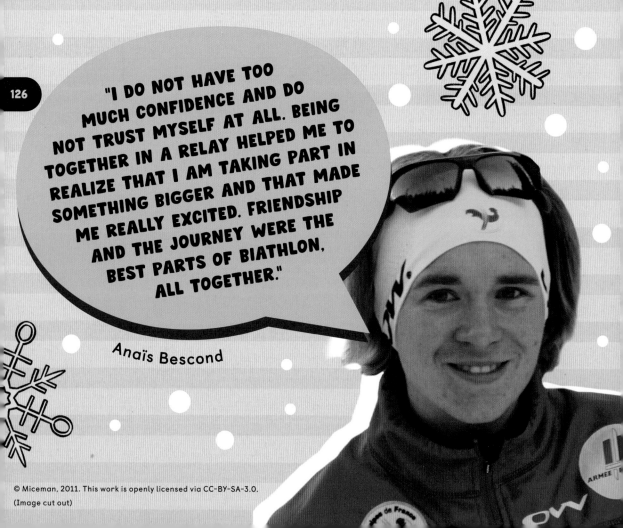

"I DO NOT HAVE TOO MUCH CONFIDENCE AND DO NOT TRUST MYSELF AT ALL. BEING TOGETHER IN A RELAY HELPED ME TO REALIZE THAT I AM TAKING PART IN SOMETHING BIGGER AND THAT MADE ME REALLY EXCITED. FRIENDSHIP AND THE JOURNEY WERE THE BEST PARTS OF BIATHLON, ALL TOGETHER."

Anaïs Bescond

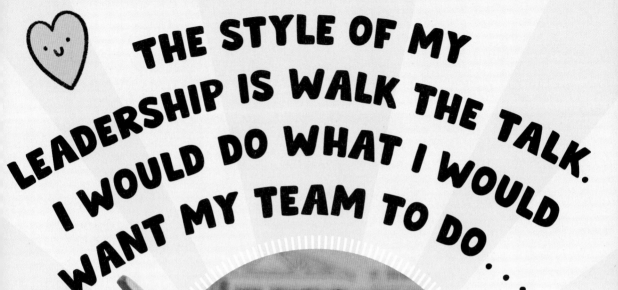

THE STYLE OF MY LEADERSHIP IS WALK THE TALK. I WOULD DO WHAT I WOULD WANT MY TEAM TO DO . . .

Captained the Indian national team from 2004 to 2022

Highest run-scorer in women's international cricket

Winner of the Khel Ratna award, India's highest sporting honour

THAT IS WHERE YOU EARN RESPECT.

Mithali Raj, Indian former cricketer

SEE IT, BE IT

TAKE A SHOT AT:

Finding people who inspire you and teach you how to enjoy sport on your own terms. Observing how others burst through barriers and are confidently themselves shows you different approaches to success. In turn, you can learn how to be a brilliant role model too.

Inspiration is the little spark of magic that allows you to explore new opportunities, keep going when things get tough and tap into your endless well of potential.

Inspiration might already be bubbling away inside you. Some days this is enough to power us through and shoot for the stars. But our inspiration occasionally runs flat. That's when others can help.

Role models are a shining beacon, illuminating the path to our sporting goals. They teach us that our dreams matter, that obstacles make us stronger and show us how we can achieve big things. Most importantly, when we see people like ourselves thriving in sport it tells us that we are in the right place.

All over the world, people are grabbing their trainers, pulling on their tracksuits and showing up in all weather conditions to practise the sport they love. Some go on to smash records and chase big ambitions, some use sport to make their communities a better place and others turn up each week to unwind with their friends.

AND BECAUSE THEY BELONG ON THE SPORTS FIELD, YOU DO TOO.

COUNTRY: Kenya

SPORT: Long-distance Running

"I know it won't be easy but I'll try my best."

AWESOME ATHLETE PERES JEPCHIRCHIR

In the rural Kenyan village of Turbo, Peres Jepchirchir ran three kilometres to school each day and she grew fast and strong. Life wasn't easy. She lived with her uncle, who adopted her after her mother died. Sometimes the family went to bed hungry, and she had to drop out of school when she was 17 because they couldn't afford the fees.

Peres was inspired by marathon world record holder, Mary Keitany. Hearing about a runner who came from a similar background helped her realise that she could make it too. She told herself that she would be just like Mary and started training hard. In 2017 she broke the half marathon world record – whilst she was pregnant! After her daughter was born, Peres set her sights on the full marathon.

It was hard, but she woke up early each day to get the miles in and pushed through the pain. In 2021 she secured her spot for the Tokyo 2020 Olympic Games, and went on to win gold. Two months later she followed this up by winning the New York City Marathon.

PERFECTLY IMPERFECT

We need to be careful that we don't look at role models like Peres and Mary and worry that we will never be as good as them. Their achievements only tell half a story:

EVERY AMAZING ATHLETE IS JUST AN ORDINARY PERSON WITH EXTRAORDINARY GOALS.

They come from places just like us, and they may not have been the most talented athlete in the class at first (I certainly wasn't), but they worked hard to achieve their goals. They tried and failed, but refused to give up no matter how tough it got.

Not everybody wants to become an Olympian, and that's okay! Role models don't want you to turn out exactly like them: knowing that you get satisfaction out of doing sport fills them with joy so, whatever your goals, you can learn tips and tricks from them. They show that it is possible to balance sport with having an education, a family or a career. They teach us that it's okay to stumble, that we don't have to listen to insecurities and that, together, we can find our place in the world.

The best thing about role models is learning that they aren't perfect:

EVERY SINGLE ONE OF US HAS FACED GINORMOUS SETBACKS. WE HAVE WEAK SPOTS THAT WE'RE ALWAYS WORKING ON – AND HAVE ACHIEVED THINGS IN SPITE OF THEM.

MY FAVOURITE ATHLETE

Who is your favourite athlete? **Phewf!**
That's a tricky decision, isn't it?

Once you've narrowed it down, find out how they got into
their sport. Print out a photograph of them and write down the
challenges they faced (and how they broke through them), who
supported them on the way and what skills helped them persevere.

Next, jot down whether there is anything you can start doing
a bit differently to help you achieve your own goals. Learning
from our role models helps us improve faster:
instead of having to discover how to become
brilliant all by ourselves we can take
inspiration from them.

FIND SOMEONE WHO INSPIRES YOU

You can totally have more than one role model, by the way. I'm inspired by EVERY athlete featured in this book – and many more! Even though they come from different sports to me, I've learned something from each of them. Your role models don't have to be famous – they might be somebody in your community from a different country or background or be a different age to you. They might be disabled (or not) or a different gender. The important thing is that they get you thinking:

Role models in the sporting world don't just wow with their talents, but teach you about how you can proudly be yourself and stand up for what you believe in.

US footballer Megan Rapinoe is a dominant force on the football pitch and she's a powerful activist off it. She uses her platform to campaign for equal rights for the LGBTQ+ community and empowers people to show up as themselves, both inside and out of sport. She also helped female footballers get paid the same as the men's team in international matches.

IF THEY DID, I CAN TOO.

DID YOU KNOW?
41% of people around the world want to see more women's sports on TV. Reporting of women's sports differs in each country and, whilst it is getting better, there is still unequal coverage between male and female events.

134

PUTTING YOURSELF OUT THERE IS HARD, BUT IT'S SO WORTH IT. I DON'T THINK ANYONE

Olympic gold medallist with the US national team (London 2012)

Two-time winner of the FIFA Women's World Cup with the US national team (2015 and 2019)

Co-captain of the US national team from 2018 to 2020

WHO HAS EVER SPOKEN OUT, OR STOOD UP OR HAD A BRAVE MOMENT, HAS REGRETTED IT.

Megan Rapinoe, American former soccer player

MATCH THAT SKILL

Here is a list of important skills that help you in and out of sport. Which role model do you think displays these really well? See if you can think of a different athlete for each one:

- **CONFIDENCE**
- **TEAMWORK**
- **PERSEVERANCE**
- **FAIRNESS AND INTEGRITY**
- **LEADERSHIP**
- **MAXIMUM EFFORT**

We can learn a lot from others, but it's important to stay true to yourself. This isn't about pretending to be somebody you're not – it's about being inspired to build on the skills you already have and learning how to become the best version of yourself.

Check out the Hall of Fame on page 90 if you need inspiration.

CREATING YOUR OWN PATH

Not all brilliant athletes get the attention they deserve. When you're the first in the world to achieve something there aren't any footsteps to follow, so what happens if we can't see what we want to become?

"DON'T TRY TO BE BETTER THAN EVERYONE ELSE, JUST TRY TO BE BETTER AT BEING YOURSELF."

Gisela Pulido

MY STORY

The whistle at the 2010 Commonwealth Games in Delhi blew and I made the mistake of looking back towards my coach. Out of the corner of my eye I saw loads of cameras pointing at me, and my focus wavered for a second. Gulp. I was about to become the first disabled person to represent Team England on the non-disabled team. History maker. Barrier breaker.

As a Paralympic athlete I felt a little bit out of my depth: I wasn't sure how I would measure up against the rest of the team. I certainly wasn't expecting to win – but I slammed in a personal best and proved I deserved my spot on the team.

In sport, you don't see many disabled athletes on non-disabled teams, but that didn't stop me dreaming about making it. I wanted to be the very best I could be, and I truly believed I could get there. I pushed myself hard, always looking for new ways to get better and when I made the team, I was determined to make the most of it.

In Delhi, I turned my attention back to the target and sucked in a deep breath. I thought of Brazilian judoka Sarah Menezes and how she always looked so calm when the pressure was on. If I sat up tall and put on my game face, just like her, then I too could deliver big results. This helped me get my focus back: I shot an awesome first arrow and I went on to win the gold medal in the team event.

Role models don't just create a signposted path for us to follow to become awesome. They teach us important skills that we can use in lots of different situations.

"PRACTICE AND REPETITION MAKE THE SECRET OF SUCCESS."

Sarah Menezes

YOU ARE A ROLE MODEL

Yes, **you**! Every time you show up to training and try your very best you are being a role model to those around you and inspiring them to do the same. Our actions matter. We learn a lot from the people around us: we don't just listen to what they say – we copy what they do. Most of the time we don't even notice we're doing this.

ACTIVITY

SPREAD A SMILE

Next time you're out and about smile at the people you meet and count how many people smile back.

That simple action can get somebody else smiling too. And who knows? That smile might have brightened up their day, so they smiled at the next person they met, and so on . . .

X4

WITH YOU EVERY STEP OF THE WAY

If you lift your teammates up with kind words, it encourages them to do the same. Role models may still get stuff wrong, but it's about showing that you can dust yourself off and still keep going, whatever challenges you face.

Be the role model you would want for yourself. Ask yourself how they would react in that situation and use this to guide your actions.

Remember that you are not alone. Look to all the incredible athletes who dug in deep and lit up the world and use their journey to inspire you because if you can see it, you can be it.

EQUALITY IS VISIBILITY. IF YOU SEE IT, YOU THINK YOU CAN GET THERE

British record holder for the 100m and 200m events, and British indoor record holder for the 60m event

Six-time World Championship medallist

First British athlete to win three medals at a single World Championship (2019)

AND YOU KNOW IT'S WORTH TRYING.

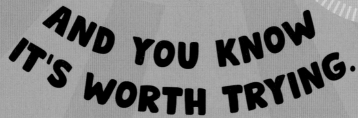

Dina Asher-Smith, British sprinter

FEELING SCARED AND DOING IT ANYWAY

TAKE A SHOT AT:

Getting out of your comfort zone and into your growth zone. This might feel super uncomfortable at first, but learning to master your fears creates a place of awesome discovery.

We all feel scared sometimes.

Fear can creep into our lives for lots of different reasons. We might worry about what others think, fear failure or believe that we aren't good enough, not just in sport but in many areas of our lives, and it's totally normal to feel like this. What we don't want, though, is for this fear to stop you shooting for the stars and staying in love with sport.

PEOPLE SAY TO ME ALL THE TIME "YOU HAVE NO FEAR." . . . I'M SCARED ALL THE TIME. YOU HAVE TO HAVE FEAR IN ORDER TO HAVE COURAGE.

First American woman to win an **Olympic medal** in judo (bronze, Beijing 2008)

Only woman to be the **champion** in both the UFC and WWE

Ronda Rousey, American wrestler and former judoka/mixed martial artist

NERVOUS ENERGY

Nerves come crashing into our lives with dry mouths, sweaty palms, jelly legs, racing hearts and that horrible sick feeling in the pit of your stomach. And then there's the emotions that come with it: the doubts and dips in confidence and feeling out of control.

Following your passions and caring about your sport (or any hobby) is never a bad thing. This just shows you how important it is to you. Once the whistle blows, this nervous energy often transforms into exhilaration.

However, nerves occasionally interfere and can cause us to stumble, make silly mistakes and overthink things.

Fear doesn't have to stop us from taking chances or from having fun. You can learn to listen to sensible fears (such as being careful when you're near deep water) and ignore those that are getting in the way. You can learn how to handle them so that you are in control and enjoy your sport in spite of them.

YOU DO THIS BY **FACING** THEM **HEAD ON**.

FACING FEARS

If our fears begin to take over, the easiest option is to take a step back and not get into a situation where stuff could go wrong. There are many, many ways to fail in sport – trust me, I've tried a lot of them. I've lost matches spectacularly, turned up to competitions a day late, dropped my equipment in a toilet . . . I can laugh at this now but at the time it was hard.

Fear is a bit like a really mean competitor. They might seem bigger and faster and stronger than you at first, but with practice and a heap of determination you can beat them.

MY STORY

The more world records I broke and more gold medals I won, the more pressure I felt to keep on winning. It was like everybody expected me to win, and if I wasn't on top form then they would think less of me.

Representing my country on home soil at the London 2012 Paralympic Games was a huge honour. It was special to have my family and friends cheering me on in the stands and the whole country behind me but, as I walked to the finals, my heart began to beat faster and I felt sick.

I might have looked as cool as a cucumber, but on the inside I was shaking-like-a-leaf kind of nervous – and this is a very good thing. Nerves mean that it really matters to you.

The buzzer blared for the last arrow, the clock started to count down and the crowd fell silent. I took a deep breath. "You can do this," I whispered to myself as I pulled my bow back and aimed at the target. It wobbled slightly in my sight and I quickly corrected it. The gold ring in the centre of the target shone brightly and I released.

"Nine," cried the commentator. Not bad but it wasn't dead centre, which meant my opponent had a chance to take the win. Time slowed, each second feeling like a minute as she readied her shot. Finally she let go, her arrow soaring, speeding, then veering up into the red. Seven points.

I HAD DONE IT.

The stadium erupted in cheers and I saw my family jumping to their feet, screaming loudly. It's difficult to describe what it feels like to win a gold medal. Pride, happiness, relief and a million other emotions mix together, as well as knowing that all my hard work had paid off.

AND STANDING ON THAT PODIUM IS A MOMENT I'LL NEVER FORGET.

FRACTURING FEAR

These three steps break down our fears. This technique works in any situation where you feel nervous. Spending a night away from home, tests at school, making new friends – try it out whenever you feel anxious.

NAME AND SHAME IT

STEP 1

Fear is the world's biggest drama llama. It takes a perfectly manageable problem and blows it up bigger than Mount Everest. The reason fear becomes so powerful is because it plays on our imagination and focuses on all the things that could go wrong instead of all the good things that could happen.

The best way to shrink a worry back down to normal size is to get it out of your head and onto paper. When you write your fear down you take its power away. It can't grow any bigger on paper, and seeing it in black and white can help you realise that your mind has been playing tricks on you.

WHAT CAN I DO TO STOP IT FROM HAPPENING?

Next, think about what you can do to stop your fear from happening in the first place. There are plenty of things you can do, like turning up to practice and listening to your coach. This takes your focus away from what could go wrong and gets you to concentrate on the things that will help you achieve your goal.

WHAT IF THE THING I'M WORRIED ABOUT HAPPENS?

It's time for Plan B. If your worst fear actually comes true – like getting hopelessly lost on an orienteering course and needing to be rescued (yes, I've done this too!) – what can you do about it? Even when things don't go to plan, you'll find that there is always a safe route out. The world won't end if we mess up our drills or lose a match – it's not as scary as we might first think. And remember, talking this through with your amazing support team can take some of the pressure off too.

THE THING THAT FEAR HATES THE MOST, THOUGH? YOU REFUSING TO LET IT SABOTAGE YOUR BIG DREAMS.

LISA BLAIR

AWESOME ATHLETE

In January 2017, Lisa Blair left Australia with an immensely dangerous journey ahead of her: she was attempting to sail around Antarctica all by herself. In unforgiving waters, hundreds of miles away from help, she wanted to break the world record by making the trip in under 102 days. Three quarters of the way around the icy polar cap, a storm hit Lisa's boat and snapped her mast. If she couldn't detach it quickly it would sink her boat. Battered by ferocious waves, she worked for hours to get it free. She did not break the record she wanted, but she became the first woman to sail around Antarctica solo.

In 2022, Lisa attempted to break the record again. Battling waves higher than five-storey buildings, she worried that her voyage might end the same way as the last. Fear was not going to stop her though, and she made it home in record time. She didn't just break the world record by seconds – she shaved 10 whole days off it!

© Corrina Ridgeway

"Yes, I felt fear of the unknown, and of what lay before me. But as I stared at the ocean, I felt like I was right where I was supposed to be."

© Corrina Ridgeway

CLIMATE ACTION NOW

Lisa Blair Sails the World

FAILURE ISN'T SCARY

Every time you step out of your comfort zone and try something new, you tell fear that it has no control over you. And yes, sometimes you fail. Failing is not the scariest thing in the world because, like Lisa, we can get back up and try again.

ACTIVITY

THE FEAR CRUSHER

Write down your worries and fears and doubts. Now grab that paper and scrunch it up into a ball, squeezing it as tightly as you can. In your mind, see those fears getting smaller and less powerful in your grip. And to add insult to injury, drop it in the recycling bin.

> "THE ONLY ONE WHO CAN TELL YOU 'YOU CAN'T WIN' IS YOU, AND YOU DON'T HAVE TO LISTEN."

Jessica Ennis-Hill, DBE

CHASING AWAY OUR INNER CRITIC

Our inner critic is that horrible little voice in the back of our mind that tells us we're not good enough, fast enough or smart enough. Everyone has one. It tries to keep you in your comfort zone which is not always helpful. Outside your comfort zone you might fail (and yes, this can feel disappointing), but you also grow and become a better athlete and a stronger person.

We get positive thoughts, neutral thoughts and negative thoughts (these are the troublemakers). They sometimes sound so believable that they pull our mood down and stop us from trying as hard as we can.

We can't tell our inner critic to pack its bags and shove it, but we can limit how much control it has over us.

ACTIVITY

TIME TO ANSWER BACK

Here's how to give backchat to these negative thoughts:

First, what are you thinking? Is it positive, neutral or negative? Stop any negative thoughts by picturing a bright red flag, flashing lights or just telling yourself "Stop!" in a stern voice. Now it's time to push back. Tell that inner critic that it's wrong, that you're not going to listen to it – and make sure you tell it why.

PUT ON YOUR GAME FACE

When you feel scared or nervous, slip on your game face and pretend to be confident. This is an awesome trick because it pushes away negative thoughts.

This can help you build real confidence, because when you step out of your comfort zone you learn more about yourself and your abilities. But please use it for short bursts only. It's important to take your game face off when you leave the pitch, pool or park because showing up as yourself where you can is always the better way.

BE BRAVE AND DO IT ANYWAY

Fear tries its hardest to keep you safe, and it knows if you don't take risks you'll be okay. Your comfort zone is a nice, safe space, but there is no room to be extraordinary there.

You succeed when you ignore the worries about what other people might think and care about what matters to you instead. Fear will chase you, but you don't have to listen to it.

If you're ever having doubts about your place in sport or your amazing abilities, question it: is this coming from a place of fear?

IF THE ANSWER IS **YES**, TAKE A STAND, **BE BRAVE** AND **DO IT ANYWAY**.

SOMETIMES YOU HAVE TO STOP BEING SCARED AND JUST GO FOR IT. EITHER IT'LL WORK OUT OR IT WON'T. THAT'S LIFE.

First female
paraplegic to complete
an **Ironman triathlon**

Competed as part of the
US rowing team at the
World Championships
(2011)

Tricia Downing, American wheelchair racer

YOU ARE AWESOME. YES, YOU!

TAKE A SH✪T AT:

Realising how awesome you are! You are more than a match to meet any challenge in your path, especially when you set clear goals and learn more about your amazing strengths and abilities.

I didn't just take part in sport to win.

Being awesome in sport isn't something that will happen in the future if you work at it. You are already awesome! You are already training and giving it your best shot. You are keeping fit, having fun and learning new skills in the process.

YES, WINNING MEDALS MADE ME HAPPY, BUT THE **JOURNEY** MADE ME **HAPPIER**.

The quiet moments in training where everything flowed. Laughing with my teammates. Travelling around the world. Positive discussions with my coaches. Exciting media opportunities. Working hard on the perfect game plan and seeing everything fall into place. This happiness ran deeper, it happened more often and lasted much longer.

If you spend all your time thinking about what you want to achieve in the future, you forget about what's going on right now. It's like looking through a telescope and seeing the horizon up close, but not being able to see what's right in front of you.

EACH TIME YOU SWING A RACKET, PASS A BALL, SAVE A GOAL OR JUMP HIGH, YOU DISCOVER MORE ABOUT YOURSELF AND YOUR BRILLIANT ABILITIES.

COUNTRY: Poland

SPORT: Table tennis

"Not everyone will become an Olympic or Paralympic champion and not everyone will win medals. But this is not the most essential. What counts is the road we, as athletes, take every day . . . The benefits are countless. If on top of that we succeed, it is remarkable."

156

NATALIA PARTYKA

Most athletes fail far more than they succeed, but Natalia Partyka from Poland defies this rule. She started playing table tennis when she was seven, practising against her older sister Sandra on the kitchen table – and she got really good at it.

She was born with an upper limb difference meaning her right arm ended at the elbow, so she joined a club for disabled athletes – and quickly realised if she worked hard, she could make it to the top. Natalia became the youngest Paralympian in history when she competed at Sydney 2000 at the age of eleven. She lost her third match and vowed to herself that she would come back stronger next time – and she did!

In Athens 2004 she won gold and silver medals. She has stayed at the top of her game for over two decades, winning more Paralympic gold medals in Beijing 2008, London 2012, Rio 2016 and Tokyo 2020. Natalia also competed at these four Olympic Games too, becoming the first table tennis player to make this crossover.

157

A GIFT THAT KEEPS ON GIVING

Sport isn't about clinching jaw-dropping wins, making unbelievable comebacks, or breaking records – even for those at the top of their game. The mood-boosting, stress-reducing, confidence-building, friendship-making benefits you gain give you space to learn more about who you are deep inside. It's a place where you can express yourself freely and explore different character traits that help you both in and out of sport.

FOLLOW YOUR HEART

What you want to achieve in sport is a very personal choice and it's up to you. There is no pressure to become the next Natalia Partyka (unless that's your plan) because there is so much else you can get out of sport.

Goals aren't just for those with big dreams. They stitch every part of your sport together, breathing life into your passions, giving you motivation and a way to communicate with your support team.

Your goals can stretch from wanting to be the best in the world, getting fitter, trying a new activity, making a difference in your community, or thinking about a career as a sports scientist, journalist, or coach. There are loads of choices, but don't worry if you aren't sure what you want to achieve yet. Try using your passions (page 18) as a guide.

THE AVON MERMAID

Lindsey Cole, from the UK, is a mermaid. That's right, a real-life mermaid, and she is on a mission to rid our waterways of pollution. In September 2021, she swam 50 miles up the river Avon wearing a colourful mermaid tail. Floating behind her support boat was a giant inflatable poo!

You see, a lot of sewage (poo) gets pumped into our rivers, killing off the wildlife. Lindsey wants companies to stop polluting and show people how we can clean up rivers, making them a nicer place for everybody to enjoy, including the creatures that call the river their home.

© Lindsey Cole

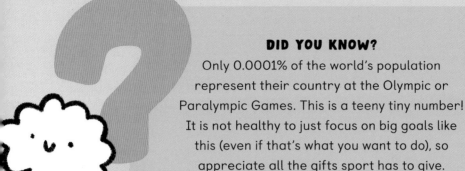

"I'M A BIG FAN OF LOOKING AFTER THIS PLANET OF OURS THAT I'VE BEEN SO LUCKY TO EXPLORE."

Lindsey Cole

MY GOALS

It's time to get your goals down onto paper.
Write down what you want to achieve in sport in a single sentence.
It could be one crazy big goal or smaller goals on things you'd like to
try or skills you want to improve, like these.

"My goal is to improve my overarm
bowling in cricket by the end of
the season and to go to the new
dodgeball club at my school."
Lottie, age 10

"My goal is to represent my
school at the cross-country
championships this year."
Orla, age 13

Now it's your turn to get
your notebook out.

My goal is to . . .

TEAM TALK

It's okay for goals to scare you a little bit. A big goal gets you out of your comfort zone and encourages you to achieve something you've never done before. When you see it on paper it feels real, which increases your commitment and makes you more determined to achieve it.

SMALL CHOICES

Whatever your goals, knowing what you want to achieve is awesome. The fun part is figuring out how to get there, and it really helps to break it down into smaller steps. If you want to run a 5k parkrun, then you're going to have to keep training to build up the distance.

Commitment is all about the small choices you make, like remembering to clean your kit, turning up to training and not giving in when it gets tough. And don't worry if you get this wrong – one bad choice won't scupper your entire plan.

That's the beauty of commitment: if you have a bad day (or even a bad week or month), you can look to your goal and find a way to get back on track.

NO MATTER WHO YOU ARE, YOU ARE NOT DETERMINED BY SOCIETAL BELIEFS. YOU ARE DETERMINED BY YOUR ASPIRATIONS, PURPOSE,

First figure skater from the United Arab Emirates to **compete internationally**

First figure skater to compete **internationally wearing a hijab**

CEO and co-founder of Emirates Skating Club in Abu Dhabi

AND YOUR PASSION. AND ONLY YOU CAN DETERMINE THAT!

Zahra Lari, Emirati figure skater

MY STORY

The problem with plans is that life doesn't always work that way . . . My archery career came walloping to an end in 2014. I didn't choose to walk away from it. I was planning on adding another gold medal to my collection in Rio 2016. My training plan was written, my alarm clock for early morning sessions was set – and WHAM! – the rules changed.

To make sure that Paralympic competition is fair, every athlete is classified to determine whether their condition is severe enough. I'd always passed this test, but the new rules meant that anybody with my impairment, CRPS, is no longer allowed to compete – and there was nothing I could do about it. Overnight I lost everything and it was heart-breaking.

But I realised something important. Even in adversity we have a choice: we can either get up or give up. Rather than being swept up by the situation, feeling helpless, I made the choice to get up.

It took a while for me to make sense of what I was feeling. My passion for sport was still there, but I had slowly fallen out of love with archery and, deep down, I was scared to admit it. This new rule change gave me the opportunity to re-examine what I truly wanted.

I believe that sport can make a difference to our lives, helping us become healthier and mentally stronger. So, I tried out loads of new ones. I've taken on challenges that pushed my body hard and raised funds for charities. I've learned new skills, made new friends and mentored some hugely talented up-and-coming athletes.

You can't avoid setbacks. You can, however, adapt your goals to keep you on target.

164

"SOMEWHERE BEHIND THE ATHLETE YOU'VE BECOME, AND THE HOURS OF PRACTICE, AND THE COACHES WHO HAVE PUSHED YOU, IS A LITTLE GIRL WHO FELL IN LOVE WITH THE GAME AND NEVER LOOKED BACK. **PLAY FOR HER.**"

Mia Hamm

MOVING THE GOALPOSTS

When you face a setback, you need to adjust the goalposts to help you keep up.

STEP 1

Check in with your compass: have a look at your big, bold goal and decide whether this setback has changed the destination or just the path to get there.

STEP 2

Write down the steps you can take to get back on track. Focus on the actions you **can** take – the things in your control – to help you recover faster. When things go wrong it does not doom us to failure. It's okay to feel disappointed or upset – acknowledge these feelings and then channel your energy into thinking up solutions.

165

TEAM TALK

I didn't have to face the classification rule change and my new purpose in sport on my own. My amazing support team were with me every step of the way, just like yours are with you. If you find yourself facing a hurdle, whether it's a massive lifechanging event or a tiny blip, reach out and ask for advice.

CELEBRATING YOU

Whilst goals point you forward and your choices keep you focused on the present, it's important to keep looking back. Celebrate how far you've come on this journey and the brilliant milestones you've achieved. This will build your confidence and show you that the choices you are making are working.

Getting better at sport isn't just about winning. It's a brilliant, beautiful place to learn how to be yourself. It's a space where laughter echoes on and off the field, where high fives seal friendships, and we get that warm satisfied glow of achievement. Best of all, you're developing important skills that help you succeed in other areas of your life too.

AND PLEASE REMEMBER THAT
YOU ARE AWESOME!

YOU HAVE EVERYTHING YOU NEED TO SUCCEED, AND YOU ARE GOOD ENOUGH, STRONG ENOUGH

Two-time Paralympic **gold medallist** (2008 and 2012)

First disabled competitor to **represent England** in a non-disabled event, winning **gold** at the Commonwealth Games

AND SMART ENOUGH TO ACHIEVE IT.

Danielle Brown MBE, British archer

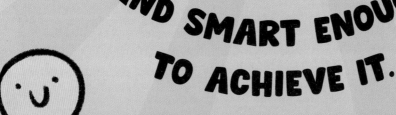

© Danielle Brown

SO MANY SPORTS: A REFERENCE GUIDE

The range of sports out there is astounding!
Are there any of these amazing activities that you'd like to try?

ARCHERY

The aim is to shoot arrows from a bow and hit the target.

BADMINTON

Players hit a shuttlecock over a net and try not to let it hit the ground.

BASEBALL

The batter tries to run around a course before the fielders get the ball back.

BASKETBALL

Teams try to score goals in hoops at opposite ends of the court.

BEACH HANDBALL

Teams throw and hit a ball into a net and try to stop the opposition from scoring.

BIATHLON

Athletes cross-country ski over hilly terrain and stop to shoot targets on the course.

BOBSLED

Involves sliding down an icy track on a sled (bob) with either two or four people.

BOXING

A combat sport where two people fight in a ring using padded gloves.

CANOEING

Paddling in a light, narrow boat. Could be racing, navigating rapids or enjoying scenery.

CRICKET

Each team takes turns to bat and the aim is to run between the wickets and score the most runs (points).

CROSS COUNTRY

A type of running race where athletes race over open countryside instead of around a track.

CURLING

Stones are slid over ice towards a target. The speed of the stones is controlled by brushing the ice with a broom.

CYCLING

Riding a bicycle. Could be racing, long-distance adventures, fun trails, mountain biking or BMX.

DISC GOLF

Throwing a flying disc into a basket. Players move around a course, tackling different distances and terrains.

DISCUS

A throwing sport where athletes throw a heavy round disc (or discus) as far as they can.

DIVING

Jumping into water from a springboard or platform, usually involving acrobatic stunts before entry.

DODGEBALL

Two teams throw a ball at each other and try to dodge getting hit. Players who get hit are eliminated.

FELL RUNNING

An extreme sport involving running a course up steep hills, often without paths to follow.

FENCING

Sword fighting in three disciplines: the foil, épée and sabre (the names of the types of blades used).

FIGURE SKATING

Ice skaters, in pairs or on their own, perform an artistic routine of jumps, spins and lifts.

FOOTBALL

Teams must get the ball to the other side of the pitch and score a goal without using their hands or arms.

FORMULA ONE

A motorsport, where teams race around tracks in specially built cars that are designed to go very fast.

FREE DIVING

Swimming as deep as you can under water whilst holding your breath.

GOLF

A game where a player uses clubs to hit a ball into a series of holes in as few strokes as possible.

GYMNASTICS

Tests an athlete's agility, balance, strength and coordination through different movements.

HEPTATHLON

A contest including the 100m hurdles, 200m sprint, high jump, shot put, long jump, javelin and 800m run.

HIGH JUMP

Athletes jump as high as they can over a bar.

HOCKEY

Players use a wooden stick to propel a ball across a pitch and into a goal at the other side.

HORSE RACING

Jockeys race a horse around a course as fast as they can.

HURDLES

An athletics event where runners have to jump over a series of obstacles – or hurdles – as fast as they can.

ICE HOCKEY

A game played in an ice rink, where players use sticks to propel a puck across the ice and into the goal.

IRONMAN

A hard-core triathlon that combines a 2.4-mile swim, 112-mile bike ride and 26.2-mile run.

JUDO

A martial art where a judoka (judo player) turns their opponent's strength against them.

KARATE

A martial art that focuses more on hand strikes and was primarily developed for self-defence.

KARTING

Racing karts around a track.

KITE SURFING

Performing tricks and big jumps on water on a small board whilst holding a parachute to power movement.

LACROSSE

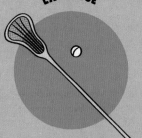

Players use a stick with a net on the end to catch and throw the ball, aiming to score goals.

LONG-DISTANCE RUNNING

Any running race longer than 3,000m. Famously includes the marathon and half marathon.

LONG JUMP

Athletes jump as far as they can to see who can go the furthest.

MERMAIDING

Swimming with a giant single flipper that looks like a mermaid's tail.

MIDDLE-DISTANCE RUNNING

Running races that range from 800m to 3,000m.

MOTOCROSS

Off-road motorbike racing on rough terrain. Athletes perform massive jumps and navigate obstacles.

MOUNTAINEERING

Hiking up mountains. Sometimes includes rock climbing and scrambling up steep, snowy slopes.

NETBALL

A non-contact ball game, where teams try to score goals in hoops at each end of the court.

ORIENTEERING

An outdoor adventure sport, using a map and a compass to navigate a course and find specific points.

PADDLEBOARDING

Standing or sitting on an inflatable board and propelling yourself through water with a paddle.

PICKLEBALL

Wooden paddles are used to hit a light ball back and forth over a net.

POLE VAULT

An athlete uses a long, flexible pole to help them jump over a high bar.

ROCK CLIMBING

Climbing up and down steep slopes. It can be done outdoors on rock faces or indoors on climbing walls.

ROLLER SKATING

Propelling yourself forwards on roller skates. Can be done for fun or used as transport.

ROWING

Propelling a boat forward using oars. Can be a single person in a boat or up to eight-person teams.

RUGBY

Teams pass the oval-shaped ball, scoring goals by getting it over the goal line or kicking it through goalposts.

SAILING

Travelling over water on a boat powered by wind. Athletes can compete in races or break epic records.

SCUBA DIVING

Divers use air tanks to explore lakes, quarries, rivers and the ocean.

SHOW JUMPING

A horse-riding event where the athlete and horse must complete a course of different jumps.

SKATEBOARDING

An action sport where athletes ride and perform tricks on a skateboard.

SKIING

Athletes use a pair of long skis to glide on snow. It can be done downhill or across hilly snow-covered areas.

SNOWBOARDING

Sliding down a snowy slope on a single ski called a snowboard.

SOFTBALL

Batters try to get around bases before the fielders get the ball back. Played with soft balls bowled underarm.

SPRINTING

Short-distance running races, including the 100m, the 200m and the 400m.

SURFING

An outdoor water sport, where athletes ride waves towards the shore by standing up on a surfboard.

SWIMMING

Moving through water using arms and legs. This can be done in a pool or in rivers, lakes or the sea.

TABLE TENNIS

Players use a paddle to hit a ball over a table-mounted net. This can be played individually or in doubles.

TAEKWONDO

This means "the art of kicking and punching" and is a martial art that teaches self-defence techniques.

TENPIN BOWLING

Rolling a heavy ball down a lane to knock over ten pins. The more pins you topple the higher the score.

TENNIS

A racket sport played on a court, with a net across the middle. The aim is to hit the ball to your opponent's side.

TRIATHLON

A long-distance race that combines three different sports – running, swimming and cycling.

UNDERWATER RUGBY

An underwater team sport, where teams try to score goals at the bottom of a pool with a heavy ball.

VOLLEYBALL

Players use hands and arms to knock a ball over the net. Can be played standing or seated.

WATER POLO

Swimmers in a pool throw a ball over a net into the opposition's goal.

WEIGHTLIFTING

Athletes lift a bar loaded with heavy weights from the ground to above their head.

WRESTLING

A combat sport where two opponents try to throw each other to the ground and pin them there.

"Some girls at school told me I was weird for playing badminton and I almost stopped going because I didn't want to be different. People shouldn't make you feel bad for doing something you enjoy. My parents helped me see that being different isn't a bad thing and doing a sport you love is worth it."

Maisie, age 12

"I always got told boxing was a sport for boys, but then a coach came to school to talk about her boxing career and she inspired me to take it up. I'm really glad because the gym is my favourite place and it makes me feel strong."

Summer, age 13

"I didn't want to try any new sports in case I looked stupid in front of everyone. It feels great when you stop putting pressure on yourself to be perfect at everything and just do it, and you wonder why you were scared in the first place."

Poppy, age 12

"I kept getting told to 'be myself', but I didn't really understand who that was. I worried whether I was being the 'right kind of me' until I learned that it's okay to find out who you are on the way."

Olivia, age 11

GO OUT THERE AND PLAY WITH ALL YOUR HEART, BECAUSE WHEN YOU LOVE YOUR SPORT,

YOU WILL ALWAYS FIND A WAY TO CONQUER CHALLENGES AND REACH YOUR LIMITLESS POTENTIAL.